W0038653

The Gordonville Grove:
Tombstones,
Tambourines,
&
Tammany Hall

The Gordonville Grove:
Tombstones,
Tambourines,
&
Tammany Hall

by

JERRY FORD

Illustrations by Don Greenwood

Copperdome Press • 2010

The Gordonville Grove: Tombstones, Tambourines, and
Tammany Hall
by Jerry Ford

Softcover: $19.00
ISBN: 978-0-9822489-8-0

First published in 2010 by Copperdome Press,
an imprint of Southeast Missouri State University Press
One University Plaza, MS 2650
Cape Girardeau, MO 637801
http://www6.semo.edu/universitypress

Copyright 2010: Jerry Ford.

Illustrations: Don Greenwood
Cover art: Don Greenwood's "The Gang at Gordonville
Grove"
Page design: Donna J. Essner
Back cover: current location of The Gordonville Grove
Cover design: Scott Lorenz, The Wright Group

Disclaimer: The opinions and stories herein are solely those
of the author. Southeast Missouri State University Press
and its imprint Copperdome Press cannot warrant any of
the information in this book and can make no guarantees
as to the accuracy of the situations and dialogue expressed.
Certain physical characteristics and other descriptive de-
tails in this book may have been embellished for the sake of
storytelling.

Acknowledgements

Susan Swartwout: the best editor/publisher in the business.

My wife Margaret: the best thing that ever happened to me and for hanging in there for the initial edit and putting up with my many hours at the word processor.

Don Greenwood: the most creative guy I know.

Steve Mosley: a much better writer than me.

Weldon Macke: Gordonville information.

Sam Unnerstall: Haarig information.

My brother Walter Joe: Ford & Sons Funeral Home.

Harold Cobb: another Ford & Sons connection.

Kenny Bender: "The Cape" connection.

Dr. Mike Bennett: Mizzou.

Jess Bolen: baseball.

Janet Robert: Cape County.

Jerry Prince: Ken Gray information.

Step-daughter Sally Bradley: for punctuation.

Step-grandson Neil Bradley: the crackerjack computer whiz.

Step-grandson Cole Bradley: the tenacious editor.

Step-daughter Karen Cain: the respectful editor.

Danielle Schlosser: my main editor.

Scott Lorenz: graphic artist extraordinaire.

Dr. Thomas Eaton and the members of my SEMO creative writing class: for enlightenment.

Also, special thanks to:

My son Keller, his wife Kara, and my granddaughter, Sydney.

My step-daughters Linda, Karen, Sally, and their families: for their support and never a dull moment.

My mother-in-law Lexie Burke: for having Margaret.

My brother-in-law Louis Watkins: for always being there for Mac.

My friends: for their support.

My enemies: for making life interesting.

CONTENTS

Foreword

I've always loved a good laugh. There's something up-lifting about it. I feel better when I laugh. The world seems a better place when laughter is near. When I traveled to Russia for a week over 30 years ago, I had a hard time getting a Russian to laugh; occasionally I could coax a slight smile. It was as if a maudlin cloud hung over the landscape behind the Iron Curtain. I've always thought a good laugh is the greatest medicine for what ails us as individuals and as a nation. We don't do it enough. Talk radio and 24-hour television news programs are too serious. They keep us upset with mundane, insignificant issues of the second, minute, hour, and day. As a result, we lose sight of the big picture too many times, and we seem to have lost our greatest asset: the ability to laugh at ourselves.

I used to tell true stories at house parties about my experiences at our family funeral home, my orchestra, and my political career. After a couple of cocktails, I'd have people rolling on the floor in tears. They'd say, "You've got to write a book." I never thought much about the stories until a couple of years ago when our town changed its slogan from *Cape Girardeau: The City of Roses on the River*, to *Cape Girardeau: Where the River Turns a Thousand Tales*. At that point, it finally dawned on me, if I didn't write about the stories, they'd be lost forever. So, here are some I can actually put on paper. I hope you gain an appreciation of my town, its history, and its people. I hope these stories bring back memories of your own that have made your life pleasurable.

And, I hope this book makes you laugh—*a lot*!

I

Tombstones

Gordonville

The population of Gordonville, Missouri in the early '40s and '50s was about 100. To make the short eight-mile drive west from Cape Girardeau, one simply took Gordonville Road, now Route K, drove west out of town six miles to Highway 25, turned left a few yards, and turned right onto quiet Highway Z. Dipping down into a small valley, the view up the hill toward town was serene. The old schoolhouse and Tot Poe's* large two-story red brick home with two majestic oak trees in the frontyard were on the left, and Christ Lutheran Church anchored the right.

A merchant by the name of Gordon received a land grant and established the little town in the 1800s. Settled by German Lutherans, business bustled at the turn of the twentieth century as the prosperous farmers made their way to town for supplies. Even in the late '40s and early '50s, Stock's Store, Macke Farm Supply Store, Sander's Store, Kirstner's Mercantile, the Bank of Gordonville, Hilpert's Store, U.S. Post Office, and Grandpa's doctor's office, still

---

* The first time I heard Tot's name, I thought, *How odd*. Even though Dad's nickname was Doc, I didn't associate it as anything but normal. Tot's nickname was the first of many that would surround me all my life. She was about 4 feet 8 inches tall and spoke in a high squeaky voice. Her face, hands, and clothes were always crusted with dirt. Her fenced backyard was full of chickens, cats, dogs, other varmints, and not a blade of grass. She supplied the town with eggs. I was in her kitchen one time. It was cold, dark, dingy, muggy, and smelled of coal oil. I never went back. I always think of Tot when I hear old-timers speak of the good-ole-days: no running water, no central heat, no air conditioning, hardly any electricity, and those famous half-moon outhouses.

anchored the highway through town. Most residents lived one block north of the highway on Albert, known as the upper road.

Gordonville was the only town in the area with street lights in those days, hooked up to the flour mill which operated until 10:00 p.m. The mill sold products under the name of Cape County Milling Company and was known as the largest producer of "soft" wheat flour west of the Mississippi River, unlike the "hard" varieties grown up north in the Dakotas to survive the harsher weather.

In 2010, Gordonville has over 400 residents. The town council expanded the borders out to Highway 25 to accommodate people from Cape and Jackson who have gradually moved there to escape the hustle and bustle of city congestion. Most businesses are gone, having succumbed to the lure of Cape, Jackson, and the area Wal-Mart Super Centers. Even Tot's house finally caved in. With growth, there is a new school, a fire station, a restaurant, and a water system. Gordonville still has its small-town flavor and, I hope, will retain it for years to come.

"Haarig"

As a result of President Thomas Jefferson's purchase
of the Louisiana Territory in 1803, French Catholic clerics
arrived in Cape Girardeau in the 1820s to establish a
school to train and educate boys for the priesthood, thereby
spreading the church influence west in the vast new territory. The success of the early school led to the building of
St. Vincent College in 1843, one of the first institutions of
higher learning west of the Mississippi River. Likewise, the
informal religious services gave birth to the building of St.
Vincent Church in 1853, the sentinel of Catholicism on the
river, adjacent to the hustle and bustle of river trade but
susceptible to Mississippi River floods.

Although the French founded the town, the Germans
settled it. They built their church and school, St. Mary's, on
a high plateau six blocks above the river in the 200 block
of South Sprigg Street. They established their businesses
around their church.

Over the decades the area was christened "Haarig" and
became Cape's second vibrant business area. (Old-timers
insisted the name derived from the sound men made
when they cleared their throats while hanging around
the saloons.) In six blocks there were St. Mary's Catholic
Church and School; St. Francis Hospital; Farmers and
Merchants Bank; Suedekum Hardware; Unnerstall Drugstore; Sunny Hill Feed & Seed; Hirsch's Midtown Mercantile; Ruh and Braun Grocery Stores; Dr.'s Fuerth, Ringland,
Stevenson, Wohlwend, Bunch, Herbert, Campbell, and
Crowe; Lando Shoe Repair; Lorberg Appliance; Hobbs Grill;

Cofer and Schade Men's Stores; Sunshine and Evans Dry Cleaners; Cape Cut-Rate Liquor Store; Southeast Savings & Loan Association; Bambi and Bunny Bread; Martin Bakery; Pure Ice Company; Orpheum Theater; a couple of barber and beauty shops; and, of course, several saloons.

Dad

Walter H. "Doc" Ford was born in Gordonville, Missouri, in 1910, along with his twin brother, Watt. Watt contracted polio at a young age and died during the great flu epidemic of 1917-1918. Old-timers said the snow never left the ground during the epidemic that entire winter, when more people died in our country than in any other year in our history. It will probably always hold the record for the biggest percentage of our population to die in a given year, unless a catastrophe of unimaginable proportion hits us. In many of our local rural church cemeteries, one can see tombstone after tombstone with the dates of 1917-1918. Ironically, that flu epidemic coincided with World War I in Europe and subsided when the "War to End All Wars" ended. Since the two events were separated by the Atlantic Ocean, I've often wondered about that strange coincidence.

Dad, like his mother, was short and broad-built. She died of pneumonia in 1943 when I was just one year old, and I have no recollection of her. Grandpa was a medical doctor, and Dad planned to follow in his footsteps until he accompanied him on a house call for an emergency appendectomy. That was the start and finish of Dad's medical career. He couldn't stomach the blood. He turned his interests to sports and became a great high-school and college athlete.

Dad was 5 foot 8 and weighed about 280 pounds. He was charismatic, pleasant looking, affable, with an ever-present warm smile, his long-sleeved, white shirt rolled up to the elbows, four-in-hand tie, and cigar. He was well known, liked, and respected throughout the area. He was a teacher and coach at May Greene Elementary School in South Cape Girardeau; ran an unsuccessful campaign for Cape Girardeau County Sheriff; was elected mayor of Cape in 1948; and opened the funeral home, Ford-Young, in November of 1949 with a partner, Ross Young, at 118 South Sprigg Street.

Business was lean during those first several years. Mr. Young became disenchanted with his investment and wanted out. Dad borrowed money from his father, and my older brother Walter Joe invested the bonus he received from signing with the Baltimore Braves professional baseball team. He bought Mr. Young's stock in 1954 and renamed the business Ford & Sons Funeral Home.

Dad was tenacious, determined to succeed. He hired an embalmer, Lowell Greer, to live above the funeral home and manage the business during the years Walter Joe was playing professional baseball. Lowell's wife, Ginny, was the sister of Jill Knox, wife of our college football coach, Kenny Knox. Knox had been a standout coach at Sikeston High School, had a successful run as coach at Southeast Missouri State College, and was a finalist in 1958 for the University of Missouri position that hired Dan Devine as its head football coach.

After several years, Lowell left for a pharmaceutical sales job in St. Louis. Dad hired several other embalmers until Walter Joe finished his baseball career, graduated from the John A. Gupton College of Embalming in Nashville, Tennessee, and joined the firm in 1957.

Throughout those lean years, Dad worked many jobs to have money to pay the hired help because the funeral home wasn't generating enough revenue. He was Mayor; he sold playground equipment; he sold lumber for Fordyce Lumber Company of Fordyce, Arkansas; and he refereed high-school football and basketball games throughout Southeast Missouri.

During the years I worked at the funeral home, people would ask, "Are you Doc Ford's son?" When I answered, "Yes," they would invariably say, "He taught me at May Greene School" or "He threw me out of a basketball game."

Mom worked several jobs during that time, including

secretarial positions at the Missouri Employment Security Division, and Rodibaugh-Cargle Lumber Company. In addition, she was the homemaker, raising three boys. Mom and Dad never took a vacation.

There's no way I can ever fully appreciate the sacrifices they made on our behalf to survive in those early days.

Grandpa Ford

Dr. W.W. Ford, Grandpa, was a thin, dashing man at a little over six feet tall. He attended the University of Tennessee Medical School in Nashville right before the turn of the century. To get there, his father drove him in a buggy from Oak Ridge, Missouri, about fifteen miles north of Cape Girardeau, to the old Houck Railroad at Jackson where Grandpa boarded the train to Nashville; quite a feat in those olden days.

Upon graduation from the two 6-month regimens at the university, he set up his practice in the bustling lumber town of Allenville, Missouri, a few miles southwest of Gordonville. His cousin Mr. Bowman, owner of the Scott County Milling Company in Sikeston, urged him to move there, since Sikeston was becoming the hub of Scott County. But wanting to stay closer to home, he soon moved to the prosperous little town of Gordonville, eight miles west of Cape Girardeau, and established his medical practice where he served the rural community for over 60 years. He made house calls with horse and buggy, and his practice thrived. In later years, he drove a Studebaker throughout the area.

In addition to being the only doctor in town, Grandpa was the pharmacist and the U.S. Postmaster. In the early 1940s, President Franklin Delano Roosevelt appointed him postmaster because he was the only Democrat in the town. His office was out in front of his large home on the main street, an old sideboard building with a tin roof and a raised, wood-covered sidewalk. (Being from the city, I was always fascinated by Gordonville's wood-covered sidewalks.)

He lived in a stately, two-story, wood-frame house. I remember his small mantle clock over the fireplace in his living room that chimed rather loudly. When it struck on the hour, it sounded like a large grandfather clock. Even the tick-tock of the second hand reverberated throughout the room. It was known as a week clock because you could manually wind the spring, and it would run for a week. When television replaced radio as his home entertainment, his long hours of a widower passed more quickly.

My younger brother Don and I occasionally stayed with him on weekends. He was a good cook and loved the store-prepared brand of pasta he called Chef Bo-De-Ore. To pass the time better, we played whiffle ball behind the office. When we'd get lucky and loft the ball into the large walnut tree, the nuts hitting the office tin roof sounded like cherry bombs.

Tears swelled in my eyes as I looked through the rear window at him the last time Dad picked us up from a weekend with Grandpa. I can still feel the pain in my stomach when he waved to us as we drove away. He seemed so alone. He died in 1967 at the age of 91, having lived a full life providing medical care for his friends and neighbors for over six decades.

116 South Sprigg Street

My younger brother Don and I, born in 1945 and 1942, respectively, were war babies. WWII was raging, and having babies was sort of the patriotic thing to do, so I've been told. Our older brother, Walter Joe, was born in 1936. Don and I preceded the "baby boomers" who came after the war. Growing up in the Heartland, we were insulated from many of the national and international events of the day, but that didn't keep us from forming opinions and solutions on many subjects.

In the '40s and early '50s, in our midwest region, every town had a gathering place or two, where people passed the time of day solving the world's problems. Radio ruled. Television was just starting to catch on, but neighbors still spent time conversing with one another at almost any place that was available.

Every town had a gathering place: a barber shop; a beauty shop; a coffee shop; an old abandoned bus in the small town of Benton, Missouri, where men played the German card game Euchre; a railroad platform in East Prairie, Missouri, where Dominos was the game of choice; and other unique venues serving as the catalyst for conversation, all with their trusty radios, listening to Gabby Street, Harry Caray, Jack Buck, and the St. Louis Cardinals baseball team. Listening to the Cardinals was a religion.

Back in those days, the St. Louis Cardinals were the only team west of the Mississippi River and were the farthest south of any major league team. Propelled by their flagship the "Mighty Mox" (KMOX radio station in St. Louis), they were truly "America's team." KMOX was clear channel, meaning that no other station in America could broadcast on their frequency—1120 on the AM dial—from 6:00 p.m. to 6:00 a.m. I was told it was a security thing; in case of a national catastrophe, their signal could be heard throughout North America. Other Midwest stations were a part of the system: WHO in Des Moines, Iowa; WWL in New Orleans, Louisiana, etc. Cardinal Nation ruled.

My gathering place was 116 South Sprigg Street in Cape Girardeau, Missouri, adjacent to the north side of our funeral home located at 118 South Sprigg, where a small grove of large maple trees shaded the frontyard of the old Chostner/Lamb home that faced west on Sprigg. The trees provided plenty of comfort from the western sun throughout the afternoon and early evening. It was like an oasis nestled between the stucco wall of the funeral home on the south and the brick wall of the small strip-mall bordering the north.

The Chostner home was one of those grand, three-story houses, with a turret roof and large wrap-around porch, that lined Sprigg at the turn of the century. The four wooden steps provided easy access to the porch, large oak front door, and a swing wide enough to seat three that hung by chains from the porch ceiling—a great place for Mrs. Chostner[*] to watch the hustle and bustle along South Sprigg Street.

Those houses are almost all gone now, but in their day the finest families graced the area. On the busy street, it was in plain view by all passers-by. Under the trees were seven or eight old metal yard chairs—the kind with arms. They rocked gently back and forth like limbs of trees in a slight breeze, guided by the skill and weight of the occupant. The breeze that moved *those* chairs, however, was propelled by the hot air of the conversation.

The early '50s were quieter, slower, and simpler days for business and the town. Our family activity revolved around

---

[*] Mrs. Chostner loved to scare children by shouting, "Boo!" Her grandson, Rick Lamb, couldn't pronounce her name Elizabeth, so he substituted Izzieboo. She was known by that name all over town.

the funeral home since we were "on call" 24 hours a day, 7 days a week. Many men had time to stop, have a seat, and partake of the knowledge expounded by my father while he waited for the funeral-home phone to ring.

He was, after all, the mayor, and everyone wanted to talk to the mayor. In those days, there were no fancy city managers or professional administrators. The mayor ran the town. I listened to their conversations in the evenings, on weekends, and during the summers when I wasn't in school.

The Great Depression

My mother's parents and my great aunt and uncle fared poorly in the Great Depression. My grandfather J. Frank Masterson had been a prosperous Main-Street business-man. He was the proprietor of the Taylor, Masterson & Linson Hardware Store, and was also elected to one term as Cape County Treasurer. His family lived in a large house on Pacific Street, but the Great Depression changed all of that: they lost everything. They had two houses foreclosed on them during those turbulent years.

My great aunt and uncle, Charlie and Liz Randol (my grandmother's sister), had been overseers of the county "poor farm." Before Social Security, many indigent people had nowhere to live nor any viable means of sustenance. Some ended up residing and working on farms owned and operated by the various counties in Missouri. Uncle Charlie supervised the men tending the fields, while Aunt Liz ran the household with the help of the women boarders on Cape County's farm located on Highway 61 between Cape and Jackson. The property has since been converted into a cemetery and three parks.

I learned an appreciation for local lore at an early age, when I used to sit on my grandfather Masterson's lap or scoot a chair up close knee-to-knee as he would tell fascinating hunting stories, one after another. He shared pictures of his buddies with many animal trophies from those trips. One of his closest hunting buddies was S.P.

Dalton of Missouri's Supreme Court and brother of a future Governor.

I sat spellbound by his stories as I looked at his pinned-up shirt on his left arm. On a cold, snowy day, his rifle had slipped off an icy stump, discharged, and blew off his hand and part of his forearm. As he would relate those stories, they made a lasting impression on me.

My mother's parents' home, and its atmosphere, also gave credence to the stories. The two couples, stripped of most of their worldly goods, nestled in a small, unassuming home facing east on an alley catty-corner from Knaup Floral on William Street in Cape. The house lacked the niceties of the day, but the presence of my grandparents, great aunt, and uncle gave it a warm, comfortable, soft glow.

The backyard looked like a truck farm in the middle of town. It seemed as if every inch had vegetables or flowers and many bee hives. I was always queasy watching Grandpa handle the bees with his Tuff-Nut clothes, safari hat with netting around his face and neck, and the smoke pot used to daze them, as he lifted the comb exposing the golden honey. The couple canned their food and stored it in a root cellar. Every time we visited, there was a large, cold glass of homemade tomato juice waiting for us.

They were proud people, and even though both couples had many hard, heart-breaking days (not unlike most people of that time), they never showed it to us, the grandchildren. I loved being there. It was a unique place to learn and discover.

"Peg"

R.F. "Peg" Meyer was the instrument repairman at
Shivelbine Music Store for many years. His craftsmanship
was widely known, since musicians and band directors
throughout the area brought their musical instruments
to him for adjustment. He originally owned the music
store and later sold it to the Shivelbine family. He honed
his repair proficiency by traveling to small rural towns in
Southeast Missouri and Southern Illinois, organizing school
bands.

Peg got his nickname from his rousing portrayal of Peter
Stuyvesant in a school play. He had no children of his own,
but his "kids" were the fledgling young musicians in Southeast Missouri and Southern Illinois. Peg was a great musician whose Melody Kings Orchestra performed on the old
paddlewheel boats on the Mississippi River for many years.
Peg and his orchestra are immortalized in a mural on our
"Flood Wall" that protects the Cape Girardeau downtown
business area from the mighty Mississippi River.

Peg also wrote and published two books. His first was
The Band Director's Guide to Instrument Repair. In his trav-
els to small communities, he knew band directors needed
the skills to repair horns, especially when they lived a
great distance from a repair shop. The Guide is still used
by many band directors and even university faculty as the
bible of instrument repair. His second book was titled *Back
Woods Jazz in the Twenties*, a chronicle of his experiences
as a jazz musician on the great riverboats and playing for
dances during and immediately after WWI.

Peg could spin a story or two with the best of them. He would occasionally sit down with the men under the trees at the gathering place. Peg knew Dad was born and raised in Gordonville, so one day he drove up in his Studebaker, rolled down the window—sporting his white shirt, smart bow tie, stogie in the side of his mouth—and with the ever-present mischievous twinkle in his eye, asked the men sitting under the maple trees, "What's up at the Gordonville Grove?"

Caught off guard, everyone looked at each other, laughed, and agreed that Peg's characterization of the spot was perfect. From that time forward, 116 South Sprigg Street would always be known as The Gordonville Grove.

There wasn't a better place to connect with people than sitting under the cool breeze of the large maple trees in The Grove. There, as a young boy, I witnessed or heard many of the stories in this book. Old-timers told them one right after another, and it seemed as if time stood still. I received quite an education in area history on those evenings. Most people, and certainly young boys, don't have that opportunity today. Everyone is in a big hurry, even at funeral wakes. Most people rush in and rush out, leaving little time for conversation.

Sunday mornings were big at The Grove. Those were the days before pagers, cell phones, answering machines, etc. To receive a call, you had to be on the spot near a land-line phone. We were also in the ambulance business, so we had to be close in order to give good, fast, efficient service 24 hours a day. That's how we built our funeral business. Therefore, men knew Dad was there waiting for the phone to ring, and they knew the conversation and stories would be lively. So they would drop their wives off at church and head over to The Grove. The chairs were always full.

Old-School Discipline

Dad attended elementary school in Gordonville's one-room schoolhouse that encompassed eight grades. Back in the early 1900s, many of the students were around 15 and 16 years old. Things had gotten pretty rowdy the year before, so to shape up the kids, the school board hired an elderly, silver-haired, heavy-set woman from Allen-ville, Missouri, who had the reputation of being a tough disciplinarian.

On the first day of school, the bell rang, and the kids scampered into the schoolhouse. Dad took a seat in back with the older boys. Without introducing herself, the teacher politely said, "Good morning, class, I am now going to call the roll. When I read your name, answer 'present'." She called the roll, with each youngster dutifully respond-ing, "Present." Then she came to Buck. He was a big ole boy and about the oldest in the class, having been passed over for several years.

Upon hearing his name, he looked at his buddy to his right and slowly asked, "Whaa-doo-yaa think?" His buddy shrugged his shoulders in apparent non-response, so he answered in a long drawn-out phrase, "I—thinnk—I'mm—heere."

With that, she quietly closed her book, got up from her chair, and calmly walked down the aisle to Buck's desk. Before anyone knew what happened, she opened the palm of her hand and slapped Buck as hard as she could across his cheek, spinning him onto the floor! She then turned and regally retraced her steps to her desk. She sat down, opened her book, and called out Buck's name again. By then, Buck had unceremoniously picked himself up and returned to his seat.

He looked at his buddy and asked the same question of him, "Whaa-doo-yaa-think?" He got the same shoulder-shrug response he had received the first time. All the young kids, including Dad, looked in wide-eyed amazement and apprehension. After a short pause, Buck responded with a soft, dejected inflection, "Present."

Things got pretty calm the rest of the year in the one-room Gordonville schoolhouse.

New Star

Lowery Miller was a fixture on downtown Broadway Street. He and his partner Gene Sides owned the best men's store in town, Sides-Miller. Lowery was short in stature and always in excellent shape; if you punched him on the shoulder, it felt like a rock. He always dressed to the nines and walked with a quick step. He and Dad were great pals, having attended high school and college together, and having been teammates on the Southeast State Teacher's College (called Cape State) college basketball team as freshmen during the 1928-1929 season.

Dad was a starter and Lowery was on the bench. Dad lettered all four years in the two major sports of that time at Cape State: basketball and football. Dad started the basketball season with a bang, leading the team in scoring through the first semester. But then grades were released: he was ineligible the second semester.

The team went to Carbondale, Illinois, to play their nemesis, Carbondale Teacher's College, during the spring semester. Of course, no one knew the new players, since back then, there wasn't the instant media coverage like we have today. At half-time, Cape State was behind.

Coach Jerry Lewis looked at Dad (who had accompanied the team on the trip) and said, "Lowery, suit up." Not understanding the command, no one moved. The coach repeated his command in a loud voice, "Lowery, I said suit up," this time pointing at Dad.

So Dad suited up in Miller's uniform and played the second half as Lowery Miller. Dad led the team back from the first-half deficit and was the high-point man in the game even though he only played in the second half. The newspaper headlines on the following Monday proudly proclaimed, "Coach Finds New Star!"

Protection?

After their college days, Dad and Lowery concentrated on working and raising their families. To augment their income, they began officiating high-school basketball and football games. Girls' basketball was as popular back then as today, maybe more. Blodgett and Diehlstadt, two small rural Missouri towns just a few miles apart, were fierce rivals and were both known for their outstanding girls' teams.

One night after a tense, hard-fought buzzer-beater, Dad and Lowery walked out of their dressing room and were confronted by 200 rabid fans. Feisty Miller (Dad always said Lowery would fight at the drop of a hat) took a step forward and challenged all of them.

"We can't take on all of you, but if any two of you sons-a-bitches step forward, we'll have it out right here and now," Miller announced.

The startled crowd parted as Dad and Lowery began the walk toward their car. The old car cranked over the first time, and they were out of there. The next week in Cape, an old farmer dressed in bib overalls hollered across the street at Dad.

"Hey Doc, were you scared the other night down at Blodgett?"

"Hell yes," Dad replied.

"Well, you shouldn't have been, Doc," the ole boy responded. "I had my gang there to protect you."

With that Dad yelled back, "Why in the hell didn't you speak up?"

The Singing Duo

The Cooter brothers looked like Fagan from the movie *Oliver!* or ZZ Top. They were tall, had long beards, always dressed in long, black coats, and wide-brimmed black hats. They never talked. They walked slowly around town, one following the other a half a block apart, bent over with their hands clasped behind their backs. They lived over the Cape Cut Rate (a drugstore that sold liquor) at the intersection of Sprigg and Broadway.

Their headquarters were over in Haarig, so they would make their way every day down the five blocks past The Grove to Haarig to drink beer at one of several watering holes that occupied the area in those days. I was told the Cooter brothers would sit at opposite ends of the bar. When finished, one would motion to the other, and they would quietly rise and stroll out the door. No one ever heard them speak. They were a strange sight to a small kid like me as they walked in silence throughout the neighborhoods.

The Steimle boys were brothers who had a successful paint-contracting business. They looked a lot like Dad: short, plump, and always smiling. The Steimles came by frequently in their white, paint-stained T-shirts, pants, and shoes. From the looks of their clothes, I often wondered how much paint actually got on whatever they were supposed to be painting.

One day Ed Steimle told the most amazing story about the Cooter brothers. He claimed, as he laughed uncontrollably, that in all the years he knew them, he only heard them utter a sound once: That's when they rounded Fischer's

Food Market at the corner of West End Boulevard and Har-
mony Street, and suddenly, inexplicably, broke out in song.

Designated Driver

The Frederick brothers, Delmar and Clarence, were tall and lean. Delmar had some sort of physical problem and had a tracheotomy procedure performed years before. You could see the hole in his throat as he used an adapter to talk. He had a hard time talking and spoke in a high, strained pitch. He couldn't pronounce some letters that took a lot of air like "H's." So everyone had to listen carefully to understand him. He pronounced his "H's" as Eh. His nickname was "Eh, Watermelon." I don't know how he got the name. There were stories about young men stealing watermelons by jumping on trucks coming into town from Southeast Missouri as they labored up "Tollgate Hill" way down on South Sprigg.

When someone would holler "Eh, Watermelon," he would acknowledge by nodding and waving his hand. I don't think the two brothers had families of their own because I only saw them and their buddy Lefty together around town, and, of course, around The Grove.

Their father had been a successful plumbing contractor. When he died, they inherited a sizable estate. Now, the Frederick brothers were known to partake of "Ole John Barley Corn." In fact, they drank a lot. They were around The Grove almost every day with their drinking partner, Lefty. They were an inseparable trio. Lefty had been a pretty good pitcher in his younger years, barnstorming throughout the area. Unlike the Cooter brothers, these three guys were always in a hurry. They didn't let any dust settle around them. I often wondered where they were going in such a rush.

When the Frederick brothers got their inheritance, they hired Flo the cab driver to take them to St. Louis. We had two cab companies at that time, Carter and Flo. Flo was the only employee of her company. She was about five feet tall and five feet wide. She dressed head to toe in black, including her chauffeur's cap.

She picked the three up, along with their liquid refreshments, and Delmar would say, "Flo, take us to St. Louis."

She'd drive them to St. Louis and when they got there, Delmar would command, "Flo, take us to Cape." She'd oblige.

In fact, the story goes that she took them back and forth from Cape to St. Louis twice a day for over a week!

Flo was the original designated driver.

Keep 'Er Full

One day, Dad and I were in the back of the funeral home changing the linens on the gurney after an ambulance call. Lefty and the Frederick boys were staggering through the alley as usual. Delmar spotted Dad and yelled, "Eh, Doc!"

Dad muttered under his breath, "Oh, what now?"

Well, they all three came up to us and Delmar said, "Doc, Doc, I've got a favor to ask of you, Doc."

Dad replied, "Sure, Delmar, what can I do for you?"

Delmar replied, "Doc, Doc, when I die, Doc, I want you to put a jug up at my tombstone, Doc."

Dad answered, "Okay."

"And Doc," Delmar continued, "Doc, would you run a rubber hose from that jug down into my casket, Doc?"

"Well, yes, Delmar, I guess I could do that," he said as he winked at me. "Is there anything else, Delmar?" Dad asked, as my eyes continued to get bigger and bigger.

"Yes Doc. Put some whiskey in the jug, Doc."

"Okay, Delmar. Now, is there anything else?"

Delmar got real quiet and bumped his shoulder against Dad's and said, "Yes, Doc, keep 'er full!" At that point, they all three laughed and continued their trip back down the alley.

As they left, Dad said, "I should have asked Delmar if it would be okay if I passed the whiskey through my kidneys first!"

Ain't Got a Pot to Pee In

As I mentioned earlier, the Frederick boys were plumbers and had been raised in the trade working at times for their father, the successful plumbing contractor. When there was a plumbing problem at the jail or other city building (1948 thru 1958), Dad would have the police put out an All Points Bulletin for the Federick brothers, knowing that they were probably in a state of inebriation. The police would find them, bring them in, get the plumbing problem fixed, and then take them home. In fact, that kind of treatment (taking them home instead of locking them up) wasn't uncommon in those days; quite a difference from the way people who have had too much to drink are handled today.

Bill Mills, Chief of Police, went looking for the boys one day when there was a leak in a toilet at the police station. He found them in their typical drunken state and told them they were needed to fix the problem. He loaded them up and, as they left, Delmar (always the spokesman) asked, "Eh, Chief, do you know who owns this 'ouse, Chief?"

Bill answered, "No."

Delmar replied, "Delmar E. You know how much it's worth, Chief?"

"No," Bill responded.

"Twenty-five thousand dollars," Delmar proudly bragged. As they headed for the station Delmar commanded, "Turn here."

As they approached another house, Delmar asked the same question. "You know who owns this 'ouse, Chief?"

Bill again answered, "No."

"Delmar E." Pointing to his chest, Delmar exclaimed, "Know how much it's worth, Chief?"

Bill, playing along by this time, answered, "No."

"Fifteen thousand dollars," Delmar again proudly pronounced.

As they continued the trip to the station, they went to seven houses. Each time, the same questions and answers were given for a total of over $100,000 worth of property—a good sum of money for the early '50s.

As they rounded the corner, finally headed for the police station, Delmar popped the $64,000 question, "Eh, Chief, what do you own?"

Chief Mills, continuing the format, responded slowly, "Not . . . a . . . damn . . . thing, Delmar."

Delmar laughed and responded as they pulled into the station for the plumbing repairs, "Just as I thought. You ain't got a pot to pee in!"

Brunch?

Grampy (Hugh Ashley, Sr.) was a well-respected medical doctor. He was tall, strong, and athletic. He had been an outstanding baseball pitcher in his younger days. His son, Hugh Jr., excelled in general surgery. Their office was upstairs over Finney Drugstore in the 700 block of Broadway. In those days, it was rumored that the Finneys had an "unlimited line of credit" rating from Dunn & Bradstreet. Whatever that meant, it certainly added to the prestige of the Finney family. I never hear of that expression these days.

Down by the alley to the West in the middle of the block stood Kroger's Food Store. All the buildings along there were two stories. They all had stairwells in the back that led to the basements. Lefty and the Frederick boys spent much time there cooking and sleeping off the previous night's activities. Cooking, one might ask? They would hang around in back of the store, and the manager would provide old cabbages and other vegetables. They would start a fire in the old steel barrel and cook stew using the discarded vegetables. A delicacy, I'm sure.

Dr. W.W. Parker was president of the college, just a few blocks up the hill. Dr. A.C. McGill was chairman of the chemistry department. Both were elderly, sophisticated, learned men, respected throughout the region. The trio used to go by both men's offices every day and get a quarter each, so they could buy their daily ration of wine. Spending so much time leeching off of the administrators of the college, the Frederick boys, of course, were very close friends with them.

One particular warm afternoon Grampy was coming down the back steps of his office to make a house call. Yes—a house call. He waved to the boys who were cooking near the stairwell and Delmar hollered out, "Eh, Doc, be back early this afternoon. Doc Parker and Doc McGill will be here at 3:00 p.m. for brunch!"

Lefty's Last Rites

Since Lefty and the Frederick brothers were inseparable, it was only fitting the Frederick boys pay Lefty his last visit at our old nemesis, Haman Funeral Home, across the street from The Grove. Lefty was laid out in his finest apparel. It was probably the only time in his life he ever wore a coat and tie. The boys had been partaking as usual and were three-sheets to the wind when they arrived. They were in deep remorse over the loss of their side-kick.

They stumbled up to the casket and looked in.

After a moment of surprise, Delmar looked over at his brother and said, "Ole Lefty looks pretty good, don't 'e?"

His brother gave his usual non-response.

With that Delmar bent over the casket, opened his coat, pulled out a pint of bourbon and asked, "Eh, Lefty, 'ow 'bout a drink?"

Never one to refuse a good drink, especially a free one, Lefty instead just lay there with his hands folded in serene grace.

Not to be thwarted, Delmar leaned over again and asked, "Eh, Lefty, 'ow 'bout a drink?"

Again, Lefty just lay there in quiet repose. With that Delmar straightened up, looked at his brother, and exclaimed incredulously to the crowd assembled,

"By God, 'e is dead!"

100

In earlier times, a funeral was a social event. Friends and relatives gathered for several days. Visitations ("wakes" as the old-timers called them) at funeral homes lasted well into the night. It wasn't uncommon for seven or eight men to gather at the rear of the chapel, or if the weather was decent, go outside and sit in The Grove and talk for a couple of hours. Politics, of course, was always fair game. Jokes were spun. The national crisis of the day was quickly resolved.

One evening an elderly man coaxed our crew into a trap. He exclaimed that in a few years he'd have it made. We nodded and let him continue. He again remarked that he'd have it made in a few years. One listener bit and asked what he meant.

He replied, "In a few years, I'll be 100 years old."

We all looked in amazement. He didn't look like he was even in his middle to late eighties.

Another responded, "You don't look a day over seventy."

The old man thanked him and again retorted, "Yes, I'll have it made then."

I queried, "Why is that?"

The old man answered with a sly grin, "Well, hell, you hardly ever hear of a man dying over 100!"

The Apartment

I loved Swifty. I was a budding young trumpet player, and he called me Bix, after Bix Beiderbicke, a great trumpeter in the '20s and '30s. Swifty's favorite song was "I Can't Get Started," Bunny Berrigan's signature song. I played it every time Swifty entered a room where I was performing.

I built a six-unit apartment house and named it Vicksburg Manor. It was a three-story, brick veneer with shutters on the windows and had four big white columns on the front porch. It reminded me of the old southern plantation mansions. Several more buildings were later built around town with the same plan, but none of them had my bachelor pad on the top floor. Charlie Hutson of Hutson Furniture Store outfitted the entire apartment. It was called "Digger's Den," and Swifty liked it.

These days, many of our orchestra jobs are over early and we're home in bed by 9:00 p.m. Back in those days, my orchestra almost always played dances from 9:00 p.m. to 1:00 a.m. Swifty knew I'd most likely arrive around 2:00 a.m. Sunday morning. He would call and ask, "Eh, Bix, 'ow 'bout a drink?" I would oblige. Remember Jack Lemmon in the movie, *The Apartment*? Well, it was that kind of thing. I loaned Swifty the keys to my apartment for the afternoon.

By the way, can anyone tell me why people in an inebriated state can't pronounce "H's?" In an inebriated condition, does it take too much wind to push the air through to form the "H?" I mean, listen again to Delmar—

"'Eh, Doc" and "'Eh Chief" and "'Eh Lefty," and then, Swifty—"'Eh Bix." It's always been an enigma to me.

It was on a Tuesday, my day off. I swung by the funeral home about three o'clock. As I went through the door, I saw Harold Cobb laughing about the conversation he was having on the phone. Harold explained that he had just figured out that Swifty had been answering the funeral home phone for several hours in my apartment.

We were on call 24 hours a day. I had a phone on each side of my bed: one for personal use and the other, a funeral home extension. Having had too much to drink, Swifty was answering the funeral-home phone every time it rang. He'd say, "Hellooo" and continue with things like, "Ooh yess, I know those Ford booyz." Or, "Whoo dooo you want?" Or, "they're good ole boyz," and on and on. Thank God the incoming calls were general in nature and not emergencies. I got on the phone with him and persuaded him not to answer it anymore.

When I got home that night, the apartment was in shambles. There were notes all over the place: in the coffee can, in dresser drawers, in socks, pants pockets, the sugar bowl, everywhere that read, "Thanks, Bix. Bix, you're the greatest. Thanx!"

The Deal

This story says a lot about the early '60s concerning race relations and unsubstantiated, preconceived notions, such as the idea if you associated with blacks, you would lose business. It taught me a lot about myself, my prejudices, and the people in my town. I'm a better person today because of this historic event. Small as it may seem today, back in the early '60s, it was a milestone in our little town, and another event that lives in the annals of *The Gordonville Grove.*

I grew up in the late '40s and early '50s. Segregation was in full swing. There were two societies: black and white. As a kid, I remember black and white restrooms. I knew blacks weren't allowed in the same restaurants and other public places that I was.

My most vivid recollections of this phenomena were in the Colonial Tavern, an eating establishment on old Highway 61 that ran north and south through the west end of town. It was a popular spot in that it had good food, was strategically located, and it was open all night. It was the popular hangout for most white townspeople, hosting a coffee crowd in the morning and a coffee crowd after midnight at the conclusion of a night on the town across the river at the various Southern Illinois nightspots. Travelers at all times of the day and night were there at the Tavern.

When blacks traveling through the country between St. Louis and Memphis, Tennessee, came to Cape, they would stop at the Tavern, step inside the door, go up to the cash register at the counter, order food and return to their car outside and wait for the food to be brought outside. The proprietor would always get nervous when this would happen. His step and fidgety quirks would rise up a notch, and he'd get in high gear. This whole ritual would make me uneasy, and as I grew older it made me plain mad.

I spent a lot of time at the Tavern late at night on weekends after dance jobs. It was a good way to wind down, see friends, eat a bowl of chili (many musicians eat chili late at night after dances to help them unwind), and prepare to go home and go to bed. So I saw this ritual on a regular basis, but I truly never understood it.

The '60s were tragic. The Kennedy boys' and Martin Luther King, Jr's, assassinations were calamities that turned our world upside down. Dad, Walter Joe, and I were headed down to Memphis for Memphis Casket Company's annual weekend outing for their clients the week that Dr. Martin Luther King was gunned down.

Obviously, that party was cancelled. It was a time for reflection, if you could gather your thoughts amidst all the discord between the assassinations, race riots, the Vietnam War, student riots, etc. Things were in a hell of a mess. I had not known civil strife like that in my few years on this earth, seeing national guardsmen shooting into crowds of college kids with real bullets! It was a nightmare. You had to live in those times to completely understand the significance of this story.

In Cape Girardeau, no white funeral home had ever buried a black person in a traditional funeral setting. The only exceptions were one or two private burials of domestic help to Cape's richest families by Walther's Funeral Home. Sparks was the black funeral home, the only mortuary in the area that served African-American families.

Many black families didn't feel they were getting the kind of service they deserved. Their mortuary's price for a base metal casket and complete funeral service was over $1,000, while the white firms charged around $695. In addition, the black mortuary facilities were paltry compared to the whites. The black community wasn't getting their money's worth, and they knew it.

In 1964, at the height of racial unrest, we were building a big chapel addition to the funeral home. It would make our facilities the finest in Southeast Missouri. The addition was to the south of the main building, sparing The Grove on the north for a few years of extended life.

One day Dad, at that time a county judge, was watching Jess Sterling finish the concrete floor that was the basement of the new chapel addition. Mr. Sterling was the best concrete finisher in town. Everybody wanted him on their construction job. He was also one of the two or three most respected leaders in the black community.

As he continued to slowly move the trowel expertly across the concrete surface, he said to Dad, "Judge, would you like to have a thousand dollars, Judge?"

Dad took the ever-present cigar out of his mouth and asked, "What do you mean, Jess?"

Jess replied, "That's what they spent on Maso." Maso was a rich African-American who had recently passed on and had been serviced by the black funeral home.

"You know, Judge," he continued, "some of us better colored folk are paying for steak, and we ain't gettin' it."

With that, they had a discussion about the plight of the black community, specifically about their problems at the time of death and the fact that no white funeral home would service them. At the conclusion of their talk, Dad told Jess he would discuss it with the other funeral directors and get back to him.

Dad called all the other funeral directors together: Steinhagen, formerly Haman, Walther's, Lorberg, and Brinkopf-Howell. They were all in the same room for the first time! For some reason, funeral directors are jealous of one another and generally bitter competitors, in fact. Maybe it's the personal nature of the business.

Well, there ensued a long discussion about the problem. Everyone was scared to death that if they buried blacks, the whites would desert them. (Those preconceived notions.) Even worse, someone might open a new funeral home and take *all* the business. I know it sounds terrible, but as I said earlier, one would have to have lived at that time in a border state like Missouri to fully understand the dynamics.

Finally, they came up with a solution. Everyone agreed that each of them would serve a black family once. That way everyone would have the so-called *stigma*. After Round

54

One, the black families could call anyone they wanted. Dad was to emphasize to Mr. Sterling that they could call whomever they wanted for the first one, but then they would have to rotate funeral homes until the circle had been completed. Dad relayed the plan, and Mr. Sterling said he would report to his people, but he said he thought it would be acceptable. And so it was.

In the middle of the night several months later, one of the local hospitals called advising us of a death. The family had requested us: Ford & Sons. I was on duty and detected apprehension in the nurse's voice. Immediately recognizing the family name, I knew the time had come. I reassured the nurse and told her I'd be right there. At the hospital, I again reassured the staff that had assembled that everything was all right. This was a first for them, too. You can imagine the conversation that ensued in that early morning hospital corridor as I left with the deceased.

The next morning, I met the family and made the arrangements. I was nervous. In fact, I was a little apprehensive, not knowing what to expect. There were five people dressed very nice, like they were going to church. Everything went fine, and it was then time for them to make their casket selection. It was a beautiful brown, 18-gauge steel sealer, with a cream velvet interior. Casket, Vault, Flowers, Grave Opening, etc., totaled about $2,500. This was at a time when the average "white" funeral was around $1,200 to $1,500. After a small insurance policy, Social Security, and Veterans Benefits, there was still a balance of about $1,700. (By the way, veterans are not treated well when it comes to burial expenses: $250.)

My heart was beating fast. I didn't know how they were going to pay for the balance, and I knew Dad and Walter Joe were upstairs anxiously awaiting the outcome of this whole affair. So I asked politely a question that we never asked white families in those days: "How do you plan on taking care of the balance?"

One nice-looking gentleman responded as he reached in his pocket, "Well, Mr. Ford, we'll take care of it now." He counted out seventeen $100 bills!

I about fainted. Remember, whites generally didn't spend

this kind of money, and we had to wait many times on the lawyers to close the estates before we received payment— generally about nine months. And, of course, charging interest to the estate was completely unacceptable.

Well, I was pumped. I wrote out a receipt, thanked them, asked if there was anything else I could do, and bid them a fond farewell until the visitation two days later. Walter Joe and I took the casket around to the embalming room. Dad's eyes lit up.

Walter Joe then asked how they were going to pay for it, and I replied, "How about this," as I reached in my pocket and threw the seventeen $100 dollar bills high into the air. As they floated downward, Dad's jaw dropped. He caught his cigar, before it hit the floor, and exclaimed, "Holy Cow!"

Here was the most gratifying and most surprising aspect of the event. At the visitation we had another person laid in repose—white, of course. When we explained to the family that this was the first time in the history of the town that a white funeral home had provided public services to a black family, they actually swelled up in pride that they were a part of it.

Townspeople had the same reaction when they came to the white visitation. It was unbelievable. Their response floored us, and made us proud for them, us, and the town. We had no idea they would react that way. We had expected all kinds of fallout. It was the farthest thing from actuality. The funeral went well, and it was a humbling experience for all of us.

We had looked at it through our eyes, not giving a thought to what was going on in their eyes. After all, they had a lot on the line. This was also a first for them too. Their stakes were just as high as ours, if not higher. They wanted everything to go well. I may be the worst offender of being self-centered. But from that day forward, I've been far less critical of others than I was before this event. While I still may not be too good at this at times, I do try to see things from other people's perspective.

Now the kicker: you remember "The deal"? Every one of the funeral directors were to be called before anyone got a second call. Well, Dad went to Mr. Sterling and said, "Jess, you know the deal? Well, the deal is off. Any time your good folks want to use us, you tell them to call. We'll be more than happy to serve them in their time of bereavement." And they did.

That was an historic event at The Grove, and it was a great lesson for me. It's a story I've hardly ever told, and one I'll remember to my grave. It made me extremely proud of the citizens of Cape Girardeau.

I've been writing this book off-and-on for over four years. Today, Monday, January 20th, 2009, a remarkable event occurred. At high noon, Barack Hussein Obama, an African-American, *a black man*, was sworn in as the 44th President of our United States. Remarkable! Exhilarating! Seeing the torment of segregation as a youngster, I never thought I'd see the day, but it's here. Thank God. The younger generations got it right. They weren't scarred by our past bigotry. They saw Barack Obama as a man with solutions for their time in history. They didn't pass the torch; they relit it. *Salute*!

Never Marry For Money

Dude, a well-known Cape Girardeau businessman, was born and raised in Egypt Mills, a little German settlement of about 50 residents 15 minutes north of Cape Girardeau. He married well. His father-in-law amassed a fortune in real estate and established his own Savings & Loan Association in Haarig, two blocks south of The Grove.

On one particular hot summer's day at the funeral home, Dad and I had vacuumed the carpets, mowed the yard, pulled the weeds, and were sitting in The Grove relaxing, waiting for the phone to ring. Of course, once again, it didn't.

Every day Dude drove by in his new Cadillac, dressed in an expensive suit, tie, and hat. He honked and waved as he headed over toward his desk at his father-in-law's Savings & Loan in Haarig.

Later that day after lunch, Dad and I were still sitting in those same chairs at The Grove waiting for the phone to ring. This time, Dude drove by in his new Oldsmobile convertible with the top down, dressed in spiffy golf clothes, heading to Haarig to check in at the office before going to the country club to play a round of golf with "the boys." As he honked and waved again, Dad had enough.

He took the ever-present cigar out of his mouth and exclaimed, "Son, you see that guy going there? If he hadn't married who he married, his biggest thrill of the week would be to walk to the tavern up in Egypt Mills on a Saturday morning, drink a bottle of beer, and shoot a game of pool with his brother."

Then he admonished, "Never marry for money. But for God's sake, son, don't let it stand in your way."

The Deposit

Uncle Dewey was a retired veteran. He was the same height and weight as Dad. He wore Tuff-Nut work clothes and high-top leather boots. He was somewhat physically handicapped and walked slow—very slow. Each step he took was not over an inch or two. Due to his condition, he looked older than he probably was. He, like the Cooter brothers, lived above the Cape Cut Rate Drugstore at Broadway and Sprigg. It took Uncle Dewey several hours to go the five blocks to Haarig where he always went for his daily libation. Like the Cooter brothers, he never spoke to The Grove. As he shuffled by, he simply gave us a nod.

One summer afternoon during one of our heated discussions, we looked up and to our amazement, there sat Uncle Dewey. How he got there without us seeing him approaching was a complete mystery. After all, it's not like he saw us from down at the corner and all of a sudden ran to get a seat. He sat there a few minutes, nodded, rose slowly, and resumed his slow trek.

As we continued to talk, we noticed a strange odor as flies started to congregate in unusual numbers around the chair. As we looked in the vacated seat, a puddle of liquid had collected. He'd peed in it!

Needless to say, from that point forward we kept our eyes peeled for Uncle Dewey. We called our actions, "The Dewey Patrol." When we'd see him slowly approaching The Grove, we would grab *all* the chairs and rush to the back of the funeral home until he passed.

How's that for profiles in courage?

"Fog-ball"

Fog-ball is my lifelong friend. We grew up together, played ball together, went to high school and college together, and both belonged to the Sigma Chi Fraternity. After college, he pitched professional baseball for the St. Louis Cardinals organization. My older brother, Walter Joe, who also played professional baseball, nicknamed him Fog-ball. While Fog-ball had never met Uncle Dewey, they both had the same last name.

Occasionally, Fog-ball did some bird-dog scouting for the Cardinals. And in the line of his duties, he made a major blunder. In the 1968 World Series, the great Cardinals pitcher Bob Gibson struck out seventeen batters to break the World Series strikeout record. A couple of days before the game, a notice came to Fog-ball's house informing him he had a package at the Post Office. Several days later, when he retrieved the package, there were two tickets inside for the World Series game. One would have been for me. We could have seen history right behind home plate. I never forgave him and spent several years trying to get even.

The chance to get even came unexpectedly. On one of those muggy, sweltering, 98-degree afternoons along the Mighty Mississippi (The Grove was six blocks from the river), about 3:00 p.m., the phone finally rang at the funeral home: "Come over quickly to Bonzi Welty's. We have an emergency," the police dispatcher yelled.

Bonzi parked his "drag line" (a very large backhoe)on an empty lot just a few blocks from The Grove. Walter Joe and

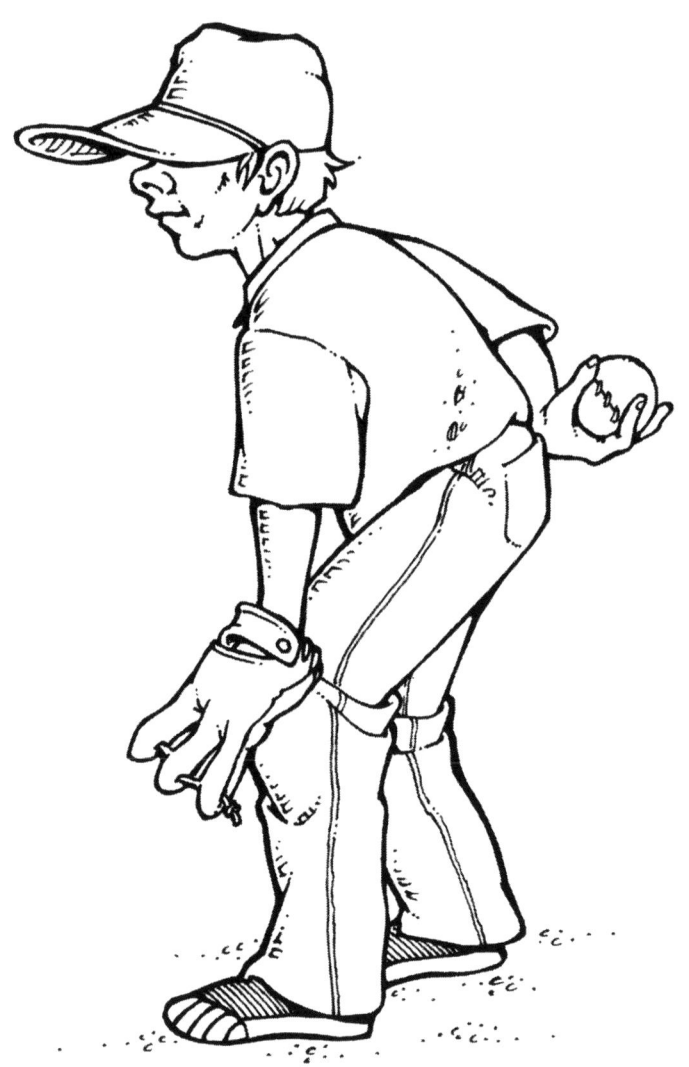

I jumped in the ambulance, with red light and siren wailing, and went over to the spot on Broadway. There to our amazement was *Uncle Dewey* lying prone on the ground, passed out in the hot sun. As we lifted him into the ambulance, a strong odor was present. Upon closer examination, we noticed that his Tuff-Nut pants had rings like the rings of a tree. He obviously had relieved himself time after time and never bathed, so the rings represented each event.

The police said they had contacted the Veteran's Hospital at Poplar Bluff (90 miles away), and they would admit him. So I took Walter Joe back to the funeral home and called Fog-ball. He wasn't busy, so he agreed to ride along and keep me company. Of course, I didn't tell him about Uncle Dewey.

At this point it wasn't an emergency because after some cool water and the air-conditioned ambulance, Uncle Dewey had stabilized. I pulled up to Fog-ball's house on Whitener Street, where we often played ball in the driveway, and honked. He ran out and I motioned him to get in back with Uncle Dewey. He innocently obliged.

Now on my way to Fog-ball's house, I closed the glass partition between the front seat and the back section (all hearses had one), rolled down the front window, and stuck my head out, even though it was almost 100 degrees, because the smell was so bad.

I quickly stepped on the gas pedal so Fog-ball couldn't get out. Peering through the rear-view mirror, I saw him nod at his yet-to-be-named fantasy Uncle. After all, they had the same last name, they just spelled it differently. So, we settled in for our one-and-one-half hour trip to Poplar Bluff.

As we left town, Fog-ball was beginning to catch on. He became extremely uncomfortable. I could read his lips through the rear-view mirror and I swear to God, I think he called me a son of a bitch! I was laughing so hard, I cried. As we came upon the big metropolis of Dutchtown, population 80, six miles west of Cape, I mercifully stopped and let him in the front compartment. After several pleasantries, we deadheaded for the "Bluff."

Upon arriving at the Veteran's Hospital, we were directed to a hallway adjacent to a nursing station until the staff could figure out what to do with Uncle Dewey. About this time a small, perky, middle-aged nurse came bouncing quickly down the hall. She grinned politely, nodded, and made a quick left turn to Uncle Dewey, who was on our cot immediately around that corner. She took a couple of steps—and stopped abruptly.

While she hadn't seen him, she obviously had smelled him. She took three steps back, looked at Uncle Dewey, then us, and inquired incredulously, "What in the hell do you have here?" I proudly replied, as I pointed to my buddy, "This is Fog-ball's Uncle Dewey!"

The nurse called an orderly and escorted the three of us to an examination room. Donning rubber gloves, masks, and gowns, we assisted the nurse cutting away his old high-top shoes and Tuff-Nut pants with the additional staff that had been summoned in to help. The clothes had to be cut off because they were so stiff with months of urine and defecation. As we cut, to our shock, there were thousands of maggots all over his legs and feet! One nurse threw up and the rest of us gagged.

The doctor called for canisters of ether to kill the maggots. It took eight canisters to kill all of them! After removing the maggots, we found the sores to be completely clean. The maggots had done their job. We then stripped him, helped him into a large handicapped shower, and hosed and scrubbed him down.

After cleaning him, providing a clean gown, and getting him back on a hospital gurney with clean linens, he looked up at us, raised his somewhat dirty palms, and exclaimed the only words I ever heard him say in all those years passing by The Grove, "You forgot my hands." With that, the cute little perky nurse yelled in a high-pitched voice, "You go straight to hell!"

A few minutes later, we finally were able to leave the hospital. We never saw Uncle Dewey again, but he lives in the annals of days gone by at The Grove. Every once in a while when Fog-ball gets too citified, living in St. Louis and all, I bring him back down to earth by inquiring, "How's your Uncle Dewey these days?"

I got my revenge.

Cherry Bombs

Another one of my buddies, Scooter, was a rather inquisitive youngster. He was always experimenting. Scooter loved cherry bombs and M-80s. You can't buy them anymore, but around the 4th of July we always made our way to Shucks Barn Fireworks Stand just past the city limits sign on Highway 61 South. It was illegal to buy fireworks in the city limits in those days.

In 1953, his dad bought his mother a brand new Pontiac hard-top car, the biggest one made at that time. During the 4th of July holiday, Scooter amused himself by lighting several of the powerful M-80s under empty gallon paint cans he found in his garage, to see how high he could blow them. A couple of days after the Fourth, he overheard his mother complaining about paint spatter she found all over her new car. He went outside and discovered the paint spatter resembled the color she had recently used to paint their kitchen.

His dad took the car down on Broadway to Roth Motors where he bought it and was told they had seen several cars with the same spatter. It had come from the primer coat being spray painted on the Mississippi River Bridge. To cover his tracks, Scooter rode his bicycle down to the bridge to check things out. While similar, the paint didn't look quite like the same color to him.

Apparently, the spray had been caught by the wind and damaged several cars. The painting company ended up paying for all the repairs, including Scooter's mother's car. He remembers hearing his mom and dad talking, neither remembering driving near the bridge. As he puts it, "I'm lucky I lived to this age." When we all think about the pranks we pulled as kids, many of us are also lucky we lived to this age.

Several years later, someone dropped a lighted cherry bomb in a commode in one of the boy's bathrooms at Central High School and blew it to smithereens. The perpetrator was never found.

Hmmm.

A Major Coup

When Dad opened the funeral home in 1949, he was well known. He was Mayor of Cape, first elected in 1948. As I said earlier, he had gained a reputation in the region as a great athlete and one of the most respected basketball and football referees in the area.

While he was well known in many circles, he wasn't known as a funeral director. When there is a death in a family, it is generally automatic to immediately call the funeral director that you have always used. In times of bereavement, newness is not comfort. As a result, it takes many years for a funeral home to establish itself.

Haman Funeral Home was right across the street from our funeral home. They did most of the business in the early '50s, especially up north of town in the little communities of Egypt Mills, Iona, Oriole, and Indian Creek. Lawrence Haman was previously the embalmer at Brinkopf Funeral Home. He possessed a good personality and was the funeral director who dealt personally with all the families. Al Brinkopf was a wealthy businessman and didn't spend too much time at the offices, which he saw as more of an investment. So Lawrence was the face of the funeral home.

Mr. Brinkopf always promised Haman he would someday make him a partner in the business. However, a shoe salesman came to town and married Mr. Brinkopf's only daughter. The name was changed to include his name, and Haman was out in the cold. He left, started his own funeral home, and immediately took business away from them.

As his business continued to grow, Haman made more inroads into his former boss's business. One Sunday afternoon after an early round of golf at the country club, the son-in-law showed up at the Trinity Lutheran Church in Egypt Mills for a funeral, in a state described by some at the time as extremely inebriated. Lawrence Haman got the majority of the business in that area from that day until The Coup.

In the early years of our business, Walter Joe and I began delivering religious calendars door to door in those little communities in October and November, and drew maps as we went. All the funeral homes were in the ambulance business, and if you gave quick and efficient service, it helped your funeral business. We heard stories of people dying of heart attacks because the funeral-home ambulances would get lost en route.

We delivered those calendars for several years. It was not uncommon to come across a group of ten to fifteen farmers butchering hogs during those cold autumn mornings. It gave us an education and a chance to converse with people we didn't know.

Once in a while we would get a call in the middle of the night, go to the maps, and rush up there in about 20 minutes. It caught on. We began, over a period of those several years, to make inroads on Haman's. Joe Schenimann appreciated our efforts. He told us several times that the people there wanted to use us, but none wanted to be the first because the old man across the street, Lawrence Haman, would see them.

Joe was a real friend. He had a great personality and walked with a limp. One leg had a brace and his foot kind of dangled when he walked. He never let his disability get in the way of his lifestyle. When you saw him coming toward you with that great big smile, you never noticed his disability. He was a respected community leader north of town in the Egypt Mills, Iona, Indian Creek, and Oriole communities. I suspect that was in part because of his positive attitude in dealing with his disability.

People admired Joe Schenimann much the same way they admired Harold "Wheels" Kuehle. I was present when Wheels was paralyzed from the waist down during a Cape

Central High School football game one cold, misty night at Houck Field on the university campus. Wheels spent time through the years fighting to change laws in order to make it more convenient for people with disabilities. During his college years, when he'd approach steps, we'd all grab his wheelchair, and up the steps we would go. Elevators were installed throughout the campus because of his advocacy. Wheels served eight terms (32 years) as our Cape County Collector.

Our major coup came one day when Joe walked in with an elderly lady, recently widowed. He introduced her and told us the story that Lawrence Haman made them go to Farmers & Merchants Bank (in Haarig) and get change for a dollar to finish paying the funeral bill. That's right, a dollar; hard to believe but true. Joe told us, "That was the last straw," and he would make sure that everyone in their rural community knew the story. From that time forward, and to this day, we serve most of the families in those little communities.

Proctor & Gamble

The old Schenimann homeplace adjoined Trail of Tears State Park.* Joe and his brother Leo worked in the maintenance department of Southeast Missouri State University. It was about a 20-minute drive from those little communities that surrounded the Park to the university. Joe was also on the Nell Holcomb School Board. The people in that rural area had joined and formed an elementary school district and were rightfully proud of their accomplishment of first-rate facilities and first-rate educational opportunities for their children close to home.

The Proctor & Gamble Company (P&G) out of Cincinnati, Ohio, wanted to buy a large tract of land just north of Trail of Tears State Park to begin a major manufacturing facility in the Nell Holcomb School District. To pull the project together was going to take many hours of negotiation between the various elected officials in the city, county, state, and the school districts, especially Nell Holcomb. Dad, the mayor, called Joe Schenimann. Joe pulled together the other leaders in the north end, and they began meeting—in secret.

Politicians don't trust the press and vice-versa. John Lloyd Blue was the editor of the *Southeast Missourian*, the largest daily newspaper in Southeast Missouri, then and now headquartered in Cape. The various parties to the nego-

---

* Trail of Tears State Park commemorates the Cherokee Indian Nation's forced march from the Carolinas to Oklahoma Reservations during the harsh winter of 1838. Cape Girardeau resident John Wescoat was mostly responsible for securing the land and ensuring the establishment of the site. For more information go to www.ngeorgia.com or www.mostateparks.com.

tiations didn't want John to spill the beans before the deal was struck.

In his defense, he was an outstanding newsman and generally cooperative in these matters. But since this was the biggest deal in the county's history, no one was taking any chances, and the meeting place—in the basement arrangement office of our funeral home—was a strict secret.

It was odd to see strangers come into the funeral home and seem to magically know where to go and find the basement stairs. They met several different days for many hours. The deal was struck, and as they say, the rest is history. Proctor & Gamble is our area's biggest employer, a great American story. Regular shift workers have amassed small fortunes in P&G stock, and P&G is a great corporate partner in our community.

Coffee

Coffee is a rallying beverage that attracts men and women alike. But where women have their card clubs and beauty shops, men are found early in the mornings at their local coffee shops. Nothing is sacred. The menu includes advice on sex, politics, religion, race, women, kids, pets, etc. There's no problem that can't be solved quickly, though not necessarily equitably. This true story is a twist to that traditional environment, but still centers around coffee.

On a hot summer's morning in the early '60s, one that is familiar to people who live along the Mississippi River with its sweltering humidity, we had a 10 o'clock funeral service in our Chapel at The Grove. Burial was to take place in the early afternoon at a country church cemetery in Kentucky. My brother took the preacher in the lead car, and I drove the hearse, while family and friends followed in their vehicles. An elderly gentleman rode with me. He was originally from the little rural Kentucky community where the interment was to take place, and he hoped to see a few of his old cronies there.

The trip to Kentucky went off without a hitch. The day was relatively uneventful, and the funeral service went fine. The old man reminisced with a few of his friends at the cemetery. The family and friends stayed to eat and visit with people who had attended the simple graveside service underneath the large oak trees behind the church. We began the return trip home.

We stopped at a small gas station in the middle of nowhere around 2:30 p.m. To our delight it included a restroom and a small café. The café had four stools at the counter and three tables for four. We were the only customers. The young waitress took our orders and went around the counter to retrieve the coffee pot.

As she returned, she overheard the preacher ask my brother, "Doc (he was called "Doc" like our Dad), do you know how I like my coffee?"

Walter Joe responded, "No."

The preacher in a rather loud voice proudly pronounced, "Hot and Often!"

With that, the waitress jokingly inquired as she approached our table, "Oh, you mean like your women?"

There was a two or three second pause, and then we broke out with spontaneous laughter. After all, we had been conducting a funeral since early morning; there obviously had not been much levity in the proceedings. Then I introduced her to the Cape Girardeau minister. I've never seen a person turn green, but I swear she did. She didn't know what to do or say. Seeing her plight, the preacher said, "That's okay, dear. If you couldn't tell, it doesn't make any difference."

Walter Joe and I kept laughing as we made eye contact with each other because there was a rumor in certain circles around town that the preacher was having an affair, and we were both thinking, *How could the waitress know?*

Major Faux Pas

My buddy Skitch sold caskets and tombstones. He called on us at the funeral home regularly, and we bought a lot of merchandise from him over the years. He was about 6'3" and weighed over 300 pounds, a hard worker and an admitted alcoholic. His face had that hard blue and red surface associated with longtime heavy drinking. When things were slow at the funeral home, I'd occasionally ride with him when he made deliveries to area funeral homes. I asked him one time how he became such a hard worker in light of his alcoholism. He told me that one day in the heat of the summer he was putting a new roof on a house. "It was 120 degrees up there, and I was about to die. I climbed off the roof and told myself if I was to live and continue drinking, I'd have to get a different job, take care of it, and not take a drink until after 5 o'clock. I've never taken a drink before 4:00 p.m. since!"

One day he was complaining about not selling any caskets to Ticky Norris. Mr. Norris, well into his late 70s, owned a funeral home in Jonesboro, Illinois, about a 30-minute drive from Cape. Ticky had always been a good customer, and Skitch was baffled by his lack of orders over several months. A year or so later he learned the answer.

Unbeknownst to Skitch, Ticky's son-in-law was John Rendleman, an extremely popular and well-respected person in that area. Rendleman also was the administrator of former Illinois Secretary of State Paul Powell's estate. In the course of his administrator duties, Mr. Rendleman discovered more than $800,000 cash in shoe boxes in

74

Secretary Powell's car trunk. He reported his find and turned the money over to authorities, which made headlines throughout Midwest newspapers.

After reading the accounts of the incident in the paper, Skitch made a sales call on Ticky and exclaimed, "Can you believe that silly son-of-a-bitch Rendleman reporting the $800,000 in cash he found in the trunk? What a dumb bastard!"

Skitch finally figured out why the orders stopped.

Sex Education

One day during a visitation, a man came in the funeral home laughing and said, "I just heard the funniest story at Lions Club, and it was about you."

"About me?" I responded.

"Yes, about you," he answered. "We were roasting our outgoing president, and Speck told this story about Kenny and his wife, although it actually happened to Speck. It brought down the house."

Speck, Kenny, and their wives were newlyweds in the early '50s and rented a large, two-story, brick house that had been turned into rental units. The house on Middle Street was right around the corner from our house on Themis Street, with adjacent backyards. All the neighborhood kids used to climb the two large maple trees in the backyard of the house. Speck lived on the second floor.

One lazy summer afternoon, Speck and his wife decided to have a little afternoon delight. They were in their amorous act, tossing about the bed, when they had a strange sensation that something wasn't copasetic. They looked toward their second-story window, and to their amazement, there I was in one of the maple trees staring into the room. As the story was related, they uncoupled, rolled onto the floor, and crawled out of the bedroom on all fours.

It was my first experience with sex, and I didn't even know it.

Purple Crackle & Colony Club

Among my Aunt Genie's many students in McClure, Illinois, were the future owners of the Purple Crackle Club and the Colony Club in East Cape Girardeau, Illinois: Joe Dodd, Miles Hill, Johnny Wilson, and Clyde "Bud" Pearce, Jr. Aunt Genie taught them, and Uncle Bill associated with them through law enforcement.

The Purple Crackle and Colony Club were swank night clubs across the river in Alexander County, Illinois, only two or three minutes across the Cape Girardeau Bridge and five minutes from The Grove. They weren't Las Vegas, but they were opulent for their time and place. Upon entering the tastefully decorated lobbies, there was a hat-check girl to greet patrons. Immediately to the left were the large lounges, generally open 24 hours a day. Vi and Eddie Keys were the lounge headliners on piano and guitar for many years at the Crackle. Chuck Hudson was the staple on organ at the bar in the neighboring Colony Club. Chuck's signature piece was "The St. Louis Blues." He would dazzle the crowd with his lightning fast feet on the bass pedals of the organ as he performed W.C. Handy's classic.

To the right were the 300-seat showrooms open 7 nights a week for dining, with dancing on Friday, Saturday, and Sunday evenings. The Big Bands of the era played there regularly. Harry James, Buddy Morrow, Duke Ellington, Guy Lombardo, Ted Lewis (my orchestra backed him for his week engagement in 1960), Louis Armstrong, Count Basie, Woody Herman, and many others made their way through the region, on to the Vapors Supper Club in Hot Springs, Arkansas, and beyond.

There was generally no cover-charge or minimum because the costs were subsidized by gambling in buildings directly behind the main showrooms. Both clubs had great food. The Crackle was known for its Chinese cuisine; the Colony Club for its more traditional American fare. Obviously, they were the focal point for entertainment in our Midwest area featuring the "name" headliners of the day to lure patrons and especially gamblers. While gambling was technically illegal, these nightclubs ran wide-open casinos. Big Bands ruled the front of the house, and Craps ruled the back!

To give insight into their operations, Joe Dodd told Dad his biggest take in the late '40s at the Colony Club was a Labor Day weekend featuring the Ralph Martirie Orchestra. He deposited over $500,000 in the Bank of Cairo on Monday morning.

In addition to those flagships, there were many other night spots in Southern Illinois including the Dawn Club, Flying Saucer, Little Villa, El Patio, and many more. All had liquor, slot machines, card games, and some had strip shows. They stayed open all night at a time when Missouri law closed restaurants and bars at midnight. Cairo, Illinois, was the epicenter, 30 miles from The Grove.

They are all long gone now. Illegal gambling was eliminated in the mid-60s with the assassination of the Kennedy brothers. Both supper clubs continued until the early '80s, and then died as the younger musical styles of rock-n-roll and country wrote the final chapter to the era. Today, when people find that you're from Cape Girardeau, instead of asking, "Is the Colony Club or the Purple Crackle still open?" they say, "Oh, the home of Rush Limbaugh." But there are two bumper stickers in Cape: One says, "Rush Is Right," the other: "Flush Rush!"

"I Feel A Pulse"

In the '50s and early '60s, we had a running battle with the Alexander County Coroner. He had a funeral home in Cairo, Illinois, about 40 minutes away from Cape, where the Mississippi and Ohio Rivers meet. The coroner system in Missouri operated on a salary and limited expenses. The Illinois system was on a per-case basis, strictly "cost plus."

Illinois law prohibited transportation of corpses across their state line without an investigative report from the Coroner. As a result, Missouri families were always stuck with a $500 to $600 minimum coroner bill if a fatality occurred in Illinois. Remember, these were the days when many complete funeral bills averaged $900 to $1,200, and ambulance service was an integral element of funeral-home operations. So when traffic fatalities occurred (and in those days they occurred fairly often with all the activity at the nightclubs between East Cape, McClure, and Cairo), it was, unfortunately, a prime area for funeral-home business.

Each time we arrived with red lights and siren blasting, there would already be a large crowd of curiosity seekers. They seemed like vultures at times. The Illinois State Patrol would call the Cape Police, and the call would be forwarded to us because The Grove was just a few blocks from the bridge. We also had many connections with the law enforcement agencies on both sides of the river. Aunt Genie taught the owners of the clubs in McClure when they were young, Dad was mayor, Walter Joe was Cape County Coroner, and I performed big band music at both the Crackle and Colony Club. Most important, we were young, aggressive, and had a history of getting to the scene "first" in those life and death situations.

On this particular run, there was a two-car accident in front of the Crackle. It had been raining, and when I arrived there were several injuries and an apparent fatality in the water-filled ditch at the side of the road. The coroner had been called. I recognized that the people in the accident were from Cape and knew the Coroner would transport the deceased back to Cairo. I loaded the injured, felt the deceased person's neck for the carotid artery, and like lightning shouted, "I feel a pulse, I feel a pulse! Hurry, give me a hand. We've got to get him to the hospital, *quick*!"

With that, people started scurrying around and helped me load the person in the ambulance, and I rushed all the victims to St. Francis Hospital in Cape (two blocks from The Grove) where they received quick, appropriate medical attention. The supposed deceased was, in fact, pronounced dead, and I saved the family at least $600 by getting them into the right state.

Tuck's Last Rites

Tuck Priest was a gambler. He and his buddy Doc (no kin to Dad) were legends not only in our area but also in Las Vegas. Back in the '40s and '50s, they were movers and shakers in the gambling world. With the local connections through the Purple Crackle and Colony Club, they always had an entrée in Las Vegas.

Tuck was a large man with gleaming white hair and rather dark, baggy eyes. He had a great family: his oldest son, Jack, was a bartender at the old Blue Note Bar & Grill on Broadway; the middle son, Big Dog, was the proprietor of the most popular college bar in town. Big Dog was also an excellent pool player, winning the National Senior 9-Ball Championship in Las Vegas one year. The youngest son is a local financial advisor, and Tuck's daughter is one of the most gorgeous creatures on the face of the earth.

Obviously, Tuck was well known in town and across the river. "Across the river" was the vernacular used to denote the Purple Crackle and the Colony Club. When the phrase was uttered, everyone knew what you were talking about. So when Tuck died, the funeral home was packed with all kinds of characters. They kind of reminded me of the members of the cast in *Guys & Dolls.*[*]

[*] Frank Loesser, the famous composer who wrote the music and lyrics to *Guys and Dolls*, visited his in-laws, the Sullivans, on many occasions here in Cape. Frankie Schott played Bridge with Mrs. Sullivan practically every week. I've never forgiven Frankie for not introducing Frank to me all those summers. I will get even with her someday, just like I did with Fog-ball. In her defense, Mr. Loesser probably wanted to rest and be incognito during his brief stays in Cape Girardeau.

The morning of Tuck's funeral, we all assembled down at Old St. Vincent's Church on the river, along with the cast of characters and employees of the Crackle and Colony Club, which included most of McClure, Illinois: Bud Pearce, Johnny Wilson, Miles Hill, Joe Dodd, "Doc" Mayfield, Lionel Thornton, Melvin Johnson, Paul Wahlberg, "Gabby" Johnson, Dick and Dorothy Wellman, "Donk" Schaefer, Tom Brennecke, Greasy Putman, and on and on, a full house.

The priest provided a classic eulogy. He was as short as he was wide. A pleasant, astute priest, he knew what he had in front of him as he perused the congregation that had gathered in the beautiful sanctuary that morning. It was the first time—or a long time—since many of these people had ever darkened a church door.

The Mass started with the usual pageantry, and then the priest began his short eulogy. He said that sometimes men of the cloth are inadequate at the time of death, that words are hard to come by. He reminded the congregation that Tuck was a card player, and if he were with us today, he'd probably say, "Pull up a chair."

He continued the eulogy with a treatise on the hereafter—what it might be like—what we might expect, etc. He repeated his thoughts about inadequacy of clergy to heal sorrow. As he continued, he reminded everyone that Tuck was a great St. Louis Cardinals baseball fan. The priest concluded, "You know, it's difficult to offer comfort in times of bereavement, and to explain the mystery of life and death, but if we asked Tuck (as he glanced heavenward), I think he would say, 'It's just a whole new ballgame'—in the name of the Father, Son, and Holy Ghost. Amen."

With that, everyone looked at each other, nodded, and smiled as if to say, *by golly, he's right. Death is a whole new ballgame.* We all left the church with a better understanding of our Christian religion than when we entered.

Turning Catholic

Dad opened a funeral home in Benton, Missouri (the county seat of Scott County), in 1954 at the request of several community leaders. Benton didn't have a funeral home, and when there was a death, families and the entire town had to travel several miles to be serviced. Walther's Funeral Home in Cape and Earl Smith in Oran serviced most of the Catholics, and Bisplinghoff in Illmo and Chaffee handled the rest. None of them would invest in a facility in Benton, even though the town had requested it of them many times.

After repeated attempts, community leaders including Wade and Bill Miller of Miller Grocery Store, Ed Terminstein and Orland Bollinger, owners of Scott County Abstract Company, and Chester Frobase, owner of the movie theater, came to Dad, and he obliged. Dad bought the old law office of Judge Spencer across the street from the court house, remodeled it, and business quickly came our way. It was convenient for the community. Bisplinghoff (later Amick-Burnett), fearing encroachment into their territory, quickly followed suit with a facility, and the race was on.

Father Schmalle was the priest at St. Denis Catholic Church in Benton. I remember him as an older and rather large, big-boned man. When we opened our funeral home, he refused to see us. Dad paid several calls on him at the Rectory, to no avail. As we began servicing families in his parish, however, he and Dad quickly became great friends. During these days, as a young boy, I gained a respect for the Catholic religion.

We didn't do much Catholic business at that time in

Cape. Remember, we were still relatively new to the town as funeral directors, and just as Brinkopf-Howell and Lorberg did most of the Lutheran business, Walther's buried most of the Catholics.

As a boy of 15, watching grown men walk up to a casket and kneel and pray in front of mourners assembled at visitations surprised me. I never saw that at my church, Centenary Methodist in Cape. The only time we kneeled was once a year at the kneeling rail for Communion. The more I observed them, the more I appreciated the humility required.

Father Schmalle died of a massive heart attack in 1957 in church during Mass. It was a devastating time for the parish. The members insisted to the area priests that we handle the service—not Walther's. The monsignor in Cape ordered a special casket, and Dad and I drove to Belleville Casket Company in Belleville, Illinois, to pick it up.

The Bollingers in Scott County are like the Smiths in most towns—they're everywhere! Harold Bollinger's wife died the same day as Father Schmalle. The Bollingers were members of St. Denis Parish, well known and well respected. You can imagine the visitations on the same evening. There were hundreds and hundreds of people. The funeral Masses for both were the next morning: Mrs. Bollinger at 9:00 a.m. and Father Schmalle at 11:00 a.m., with both committals in the cemetery behind the church.

St. Denis seats around 300 people, and there were over 500 in attendance. In addition, there were 70 to 80 priests for Father Schmalle's High Mass. Loud speakers were set up for people to hear outside. All the doors were open, and there was a solid wall of people from the church through the vestibule and outside—we were packed like sardines. It was our practice to have Dad and Walter Joe sit on the back pew on each side of the church, and I would be on the inside seat in the back center pew. At the conclusion of the service, Dad and Walter Joe would proceed down the side aisles, and I, down the middle.

Well, with this large crowd, there was no seat for me. I was relegated to the center of the vestibule where I took my place with about 500 other people, mostly adults, but close enough to direct order at the conclusion.

Father Schmalle's Mass started, and at the appropriate

time, 500 people kneeled. Now the only three non-Catholics within 100 miles were me, Walter Joe, and Dad! They were both safe in their rear pew seats. But I was stuck and standing on display with 300 in front and 200 behind. I was shook and didn't know what to do, so I just continued to stand. In a minute or so, the congregation returned to their seats or stood; I was safe. Then it happened again.

This time Monroe Bollinger, who saw my plight, stood with me. Monroe was a carpenter by trade and a drummer in a country swing band. He and his wife Marie operated M&M BBQ Drive-In. He was also a good square-dance caller. I'll never forget Monroe coming to my rescue. However, the last several times they kneeled, I acquiesced and kneeled with them. I buckled under the pressure.

Ben Meyer was the maintenance man at the church, a complex consisting of a school, church, rectory, cemetery, and several acres. He was a busy yet quiet man, who was always nice to me. He, like many Catholics of the day, had a large family. His seat at church was generally in the rear where he could observe the proceedings and toll the bell at the conclusion. After the services, he approached Dad as people were leaving the cemetery and remarked after observing my kneeling during the Mass, "You know, Doc, I think we almost made a Catholic out of Jerry this morning!"

II

Tambourines

Musicians

We all like to have friends and be appreciated. I pride myself in the many friends I've made over the years. My brother Don was my best friend. We created a special bond performing music throughout the Midwest for years. In our style, we had the freedom to place our thoughts, ideas, creativity, personality, intellect, and humor—our whole being— into the improvised interpretation of the music. Our bond was in America's gift to the world: Jazz.

Most of us need anchors to provide balance in our lives. We all have ups and downs in life and need something or someone to help keep us grounded. Rick Warren discusses the issue in his best-selling book *The Purpose Driven Life.* Your relationship with God is central in your beliefs. In addition to faith, combinations of family, work, politics, sports, hobbies, recreation, art, books, and others help me. Besides Don, I've been fortunate to also have other people along the way, especially my parents, my wife Margaret, my son Keller, and those many friends. In addition, my trumpet and music have always been with me. They've all kept me half sane through trials and tribulations that have passed my way. As Hillary Clinton states it, "It takes a village."

$60 / $40

Gordonville had a one-room schoolhouse consisting of eight grades. Upon graduation in the early 1900s, it was generally the custom for boys to go to work on local farms, while some of the girls were sent to St. Louis to be hired as domestic help for wealthy families.

Grandpa didn't want his daughters to be domestic help. He worked out a deal with President Serena at the Teacher's College in Cape Girardeau for the girls to stay at Leming Hall Dormitory on the campus and go to high school at the College Training School. He moved Aunt Genie up a grade so she and Aunt Neva could attend together. The training school was a high school located on the college campus that augmented its staff with college students who were being trained as teachers.

Grandpa would drive the girls eight miles to school early on Monday mornings and pick them up late on Friday afternoons. He did this for four years. When it was time for college, he enrolled them, and they continued to live in Leming Hall for another four years, except for Aunt Neva, who married Elmore Kassel, received a temporary teaching certificate, and left after two years. She finished her four-year degree during ensuing summers. Aunt Genie stayed the full four years.

Aunt Genie said it wasn't uncommon for college students and returning teachers to exclaim, "Aren't you Ford girls ever going to leave here?" I suspect they still hold the record for longevity as students in the college dormitories, if not Aunt Neva with six years, certainly Aunt Genie with eight.

Aunt Genie immediately got a job teaching across the river in nearby McClure, Illinois, about five miles east of Cape Girardeau. She married a local McClure man with political connections, Bill Abernathie. Uncle Bill was also a teacher. Later he became a deputy sheriff. Over the years he became an influential person in and around Southern Illinois and the capitol in Springfield, where, on the side, he operated the polygraph (lie detector) machine for the Illinois Highway Patrol.

Uncle Elmore was a jeweler by trade, and he relished a deal. He was short, slightly built, sporting a shiny, bald head, and was a bundle of energy. At 5' 7" and 160 pounds, he was constantly on the move. He made a sound between his teeth somewhat like a baby sucking on a pacifier to proudly call attention to his gold tooth. In addition, he scurried around repeating in a melodic, rapid-fire fashion, his signature, "*Ta doo, ta doo.*" That's right, "*Ta doo, ta doo!*" The sound was made by forcing the tip of his tongue fast behind his front teeth—like a Gatling gun!

Uncle Elmore was a great clarinetist, which is something you hear from time to time about musicians. Sometimes it's correct, and sometimes it's not. In Uncle Elmore's case, it was true. He came from a musical family and played throughout the Midwest, including the paddle-wheel boats up and down the Mississippi River. He played with Peg Meyer and the Melody Kings and is memorialized with them on the painted mural down on the Cape floodwall.

He played "first chair" clarinet in the Cape Girardeau Municipal Band for more than 40 years. We've had some great players through the years on the first chair, including high-school band directors and college professors with degrees in performance. None could match Uncle Elmore. He zipped through those old, classic, overture violin-cadenza transcriptions, such as Franz von Suppe's *Light Cavalry* and *Morning, Noon and Night in Vienna*, on his clarinet like you never heard! He even embellished them with humorous licks like "Popeye the Sailor Man."

One of his buddies in the Municipal Band was Bob Schultz, an outstanding baritone horn player. Bob's brother Jack was a professional piano player and the Dean of Admissions at the Washington University Medical School in St. Louis. Jack was one of several great pianists who originated in Cape. Jerry Abernathy (no kin to Uncle Bill) performed in Los Angeles and Las Vegas for years. Bob and Jack's father, Louis J. Schultz, was our Superintendent of Schools for many years and had a school named after him in Cape. The most famous musician, however, was Jess Stacy, who was Benny Goodman's side man during the Big Band Era. I never heard a baritone horn part played very well in high school or college, so I was surprised to hear my first trumpet part being played across the room by a baritone horn in the Municipal Band. The city band owned a baritone horn, and Bob would play it during the 14-week summer concert series, then lay it down until the next year. He would pick it up after the nine-month layoff and start up again as if he never left it. It was uncanny that a brass player could do that. Good brass players have to play every day to keep their embouchure in that kind of shape; not Bob Schultz.

Well, Bob told me this Uncle Elmore story. It was about one of Elmore's many $60/$40 jobs. (A "job" in musician's vernacular means an engagement, a dance, a reception, etc.) Bob answered the phone one day, and it was Uncle Elmore on the other end: "Got a job—*ta doo*—got a job—*ta doo.*"

Jack, recognizing the vocabulary of Elmore, asked, "Where is it?"

Elmore continued, "Anna, Illinois—*ta doo, ta doo.*"

"When?" Jack asked.

"Next Saturday—*ta doo, ta doo.*"

"What's it paying?" Jack quizzed.

Elmore announced, "$60/$40—*ta doo*—$60/$40!"

Jack shouted, "What do you mean $60/$40?"

Elmore concluded, "I get $60 dollars, you guys *split* $40!"

My First Performance

My 13-piece, swing, dance orchestra has performed throughout the Midwest for over 50 years. We specialize in music of the Great American Songbook. I began at a very young age. When I heard a trumpet on the radio, I pestered my Dad and Tony Carosello, the high-school band director, until they let me begin taking lessons in the fourth grade.

Harry Ranch was a trumpet player who led a cabaret show band combo in the late '40s, '50s, and '60s similar to Louis Prima and Keely Smith. He headquartered in Florida and made an annual swing through the lounges of Las Vegas and the Midwest. He was a staple each summer at the Colony Club, the night club in East Cape, Illinois, only two minutes across the bridge from The Grove.

The year was 1953; I was in the fifth grade, a budding young trumpet player. Harry had gambled himself into substantial debt and had to prolong his stay. He moved his wife and daughter into the Idan-Ha Hotel (one block from our house) in downtown Cape, enrolled his daughter in the fourth grade at Lorimier School, and continued to perform at the Colony Club to pay off his debt.

During their two-month stay, his daughter had a birthday party over at the Colony Club. I was invited to perform, my first professional performance. We had dinner with the usual cake and ice cream. We also had fun with all kinds of hats, whistles, funny little noisemaker gadgets, etc. Years later, as I began playing in dance orchestras, I realized the toys were leftover New Year's Eve party favors.

As the evening progressed, the sun went down, table

candles were lit, other people began filtering in the 300-plus room for the night's meal and entertainment. It was time for us to go home. But before we left, Harry had the 100 or more patrons sing "Happy Birthday" to his daughter, then he introduced me. I proceeded to set up my music stand and music in the middle of the dance floor, and got ready to play my trumpet solo "Tenderly"—or so I thought.

The house lights dimmed, spotlights were turned on, and Harry looked at me and proclaimed, "Jerry, you're not dressed for the occasion." He placed a red mop wig on my head and said, "We're going to give you a four-bar introduction, and then you play."

Well, that got a few laughs from the crowd. As I started to play, the drummer crashed the cymbals, the trombone player "smeared," the saxophonist "honked" his horn, as the band fell apart! As the crowd laughed more, Harry placed a six-foot-long circus tie around my neck, and we started again.

To my surprise, the same thing happened. The band fell apart again. This time Harry placed a flop-eared felt hat on me, and we tried again, to no avail. By this time he had the crowd in tears, literally rolling in the aisles. Here I am, a fifth grader, holding a trumpet about as big as me, standing in the middle of the floor with spotlights on me, sporting a red wig, circus tie, and flop-eared hat. It nearly caused a riot!

Then he proclaimed with all sincerity, "Jerry, this time we really are going to start." With that, I took a deep breath and prepared to blow the roof off the place. At that point— yes, you guessed it—he stopped again.

This time he sauntered up to me with a big smile and placed a potty on the floor at my feet and said, "Jerry, this is just in case." With that, those who weren't on the floor laughing joined the rest of the crowd. Finally, on the fifth try, we got it right.

That was my introduction to showbiz.

Comeuppance

My buddy Tommy Stovall and I were pretty good trumpet players in junior-high school. We did quite well on the talent-show circuit one summer between the sixth and seventh grades. Our big number was a trumpet duet, "Yes Sir, That's My Baby." We won several of the competitions with our peppy rendition. When we didn't win first place, we were usually trumped (no pun intended) by Lou Hobbs, a boy of our age who played the guitar and sang country music. His hit was the old Hank Williams classic, "Your Cheat'n Heart."

The pinnacle of the talent shows in those days was the Labor Day Cape Girardeau American Legion picnic in Capaha Park. Those were the days before interstate highways, chain motels, and the development that followed them. The two big hotels in downtown Cape Girardeau were the Marquette and Idan-Ha.* They were across the street from one another, one block from my home on Themis Street.

Unbeknownst to us at that time, the Legion members would go to the hotels and solicit traveling salesmen to be judges of the talent show. Their enticement and remuneration were all they could eat and drink."

We were terrific on stage that evening—or so we thought.

---

* Years later, the Idan-Ha burned, and after decades of neglect, the Marquette was restored and converted into a state office building. The Marquette, the new Federal Courthouse Building, River Campus for the Visual and Performing Arts on the old St. Vincent's Seminary grounds, and new four-lane Bill Emerson Memorial Mississippi River Bridge have started a more than $250 million renaissance of the entire downtown area of Cape Girardeau.

Lou gave his usual good rendition; Ole Hank would have been proud. At the conclusion, Tommy and I confidently stood in the wings waiting for the announcement that we had won another $25 savings bond. And then we got our comeuppance.

Third place went to Lou Hobbs. Third place? Lou always got first or second. Then came the second-place announcement: "Now before we announce second place, the judges want us to say these boys were really good," the emcee proclaimed. Second place went to none other than Tommy Stovall and Jerry Ford, with the trumpet duet, "Yes Sir, That's My Baby."

I thought, *Second place? They've got to be kidding. What's going on?* Well, there were these three little girls in leotards who flipped across the stage. The judges (probably in their inebriated state) thought the little girls were cute, so they awarded them *first place*! Even though we were devastated, if the truth be known, the little girls were probably better.

We never entered another talent show.

Church Blast

Musicians have always been in demand for Sunday church services. With the advent of mega churches, they are even more sought-after to fill the orchestral sections. Brass instruments are always good for church. Centenary United Methodist in Cape Girardeau had a very large sanctuary before they remodeled. Wood floors and stucco ceilings make for great, loud sounds.

On this particular Sunday in 1957, when I was a sophomore in high school, the choir director wanted a brass ensemble for the offertory. I suspect he felt a brass choir in all its glory might move the congregation to dig a little deeper during the passing of the collection plates. At any rate, we had three trumpets: Tony Carosello, Al Estes, and myself; two trombones: Dr. Fred Goodwin and Bill Headrick; one French horn: Ted Miller; tympani: Dr. T. Donley Thomas; and the phantom of the opera at the organ: Dr. Dan Cotner. It was quite a powerful assemblage.

Tony was my high-school band director. He was an outstanding educator and trumpet player. Al Estes was probably the best trumpeter to ever come out of Central High School, and that's saying a lot. Tony also taught him. Dr. Fred Goodwin was Dean of Humanities at the University and a fine jazz trombonist. Bill Headrick was an outstanding high-school trombone player. He would have been a great one, but he laid down his trombone in college, picked up a paint brush, and became an art instructor. Ted Miller, a college student at the time, later played in the Nashville Symphony for many years. T. Donley was a musicologist on

99

the University music staff, and Dr. Dan Cotner, a dentist, is still blowing the roof off local churches after all these years! So when I say it was a powerful assemblage, it was indeed.

When the time came for us to play, as the collection plates were being distributed, I expected Tony Carosello to call off the four-beat cadence with a soft whisper—NOT! He stomped his shoe with four loud beats on the hardwood floor of the choir loft. We reared back, took a deep breath, and blasted the fortissimo opening with all we had. The entire congregation jumped. One lady screamed, her program flying through the air as we proceeded to take the roof off the place. The Holy Ghost was definitely present.

For several years afterwards, when we'd think of it, we would ask each other, "Has anyone from Centenary invited us back?"

No one ever did.

Tup's Magic Drive

Tup liked to drink, what I would call a gentleman's alcoholic. He generally drank in the evenings. He had the capacity to not let it interfere with his business, and he never got belligerent as far as I knew.

One night Tup and some of his buddies were at the Purple Crackle. The Crackle had music seven nights a week, so it was always a gathering place. It was late, and Tup had too much to drink. The boys knew he was in no shape to drive across the narrow bridge, so they drove him thru Haarig by The Grove to his home. They deposited him at his front door, rang the doorbell, and scooted back into their car. They didn't want to face his wife.

On the way back to the Crackle as the boys passed The Grove, they stopped in Haarig at the Cape Cut Rate Liquor Store to buy a pack of cigarettes. When they returned to the Crackle bar, to their astonishment, there sat Tup!

He raised his drink and exclaimed, "What kept you, boys?"

He obviously had gone straight to his other car, and magically maneuvered the very narrow two-lane bridge constructed in 1927 back across the river while the boys stopped for cigarettes.

"Buddy"

My friend Buddy was a bar-room piano player. He had traveled around the country playing in various orchestras, so he knew the music literature by memory. His style of playing resembled the famous Errol Garner. He would flap the four fingers of his right hand on the bar to imitate Errol's style when expounding on one of Errol's hits like "Misty."

Buddy was a fixture at the Purple Crackle. He played in the main showroom with the Bill Brandt Quartet on Friday nights and the Herb Suedekum Orchestra on Saturday nights, so he had great exposure to area patrons. He also lived on the grounds in a tiny, round-humped trailer. It was a midget version of those silver Airstreams. There was hardly enough room to turn around, let alone sleep. Bud Pearce, the owner of the Crackle, took him in and watched over him, like he did many others over the years in East Cape. Buddy was the chief gardener, tree planter, vacuum sweeper, custodian, bottle washer, security guard (kind of), and any other odd job that needed to be done around the place. He could even cook a mean breakfast.

Bud Pearce called the funeral home one night and informed us they had found Buddy dead in his trailer at the back of the Crackle. So Walter Joe and I took the hearse over to pick him up.

In those days, musicians usually were paid about $30 per night in cash. Upon arrival, Bud asked us to help sort through Buddy's belongings. We began discovering $20 dollar bills. They were everywhere: in pockets, in books, under the mattress of his bed, in coffee cans, everywhere. He obviously spent the $10s occasionally and saved the $20s. He really never needed too much money because, again, Bud took care of him. He ate and drank free at the Crackle. He didn't need many clothes. He didn't travel much, although he had an old beat-up car. So he just stashed the $20s in his trailer.

At some point, I turned to Bud with two hands full of $20 bills. He asked, "Jerry, how much do you have there?"

I replied, "I don't know yet, but there must be well over a thousand dollars."

He then asked, "How much would it cost to put ole Buddy away first class—like in a solid copper casket and a good vault?"

I replied, "Oh, somewhere around $2,500."

Bud said, "Do it, and I'll make up the difference. Buddy deserves a good funeral." So we did.

The evening visitation took place two nights later. There was a big crowd in attendance. All the band leaders, musicians, gamblers, drinkers, pit bosses, dancers, bus boys, waitresses, hat-check girls, and regular patrons were present. It was quite a show, everyone reminiscing about the good times across the river in the '30s, '40s, and '50s during the heyday of the Big Bands. The chapel was abuzz with the news that Bud had buried Buddy in style. It was another in the long line of charitable acts that Bud Pearce had fulfilled, not unlike the Drury brothers of the national hotel chain, whom I've seen make charitable gestures for their employees during their bereavement. It added to Bud's legacy and made great conversation at the wake. Most people never really notice the casket at a funeral, but on this evening, everyone was admiring the facade. Laid out in the finest available, Buddy never looked better. It was a regal sight!

Now enters Lionel Thornton, tall and secretive. He was the main bartender at the Colony Club, then the Crackle, then the Elk's Club, and in his final years, a maitre d' at Denny's. You can trace the demise of gambling and nightclubs in those days with his employment. Lionel reminded me of Sheldon Leonard, the "Hood" in the old Jack Benny TV shows. Sheldon was dark skinned, talked with a

Brooklyn accent, and always gave Jack advice as to what to and what not to buy in the grocery store. If Jack was about to buy green beans, there Sheldon would stand, dressed in a black suit, black shirt, and white tie, shaking his head from side to side admonishing Jack, "Do not buy the green beans; buy the butter beans," and so on. He made an instant impression on me every time he appeared on the show. As many know, Leonard ended up as the producer of *The Andy Griffith Show*—one of the greatest, most beloved TV shows of all time.

It wasn't the Brooklyn accent that connected Lionel and Sheldon, it was Sheldon's secretive way of talking, his inflections. Lionel had them down perfectly. He talked out of the side of his mouth very softly, and you had to really concentrate to hear him plainly. So there was Lionel, standing beside me in the rear of our Chapel at The Grove, perusing the congregation that had gathered for Buddy's wake. He leaned over to me, hands clasped in front of him in serene respect, and muttered out of the side of his mouth with Sheldon Leonard's accent, "Jerry, do you know the definition of a hypocrite?"

I softly answered, "No."

He leaned closer, bumped my shoulder with his, and answered even quieter, "That's an undertaker who can look sober at a $10,000 funeral!"

He never smiled. He swung back to his usual erect position and continued to review the proceedings with unabashed serenity. I followed suit, biting my lip to keep from laughing out loud.

Woody Herman

Woody Herman and his Thundering Herd were one of the great classic orchestras of the Big Band Era. I had the good fortune of hearing them live on four separate occasions. They would start with their theme song "Blue Flame," with its slow, mysterious, almost African feel, showcasing Woody's haunting, wailing clarinet. It was just the opposite of the rhythmic, brassy, powerful style that the nickname "Thundering Herd" exemplified. The band would usually segue immediately into "Four Brothers," featuring the skill and blazing technique of his great saxophone section. And then you hung on to your seats the rest of the evening for the thrill, energy, and sheer power of The Thundering Herd!

As is the case at times with musicians, Woody's music exemplified his personality. He was a legend among musicians for being a tyrant, especially to the brass, and most especially to the lead trumpet player. His swing arrangements required legendary feats from the lead trumpeter. This temperament many times carried over to his interaction with patrons.

One December night in the '60s, he was performing at the Purple Crackle Club for the Cape Girardeau Rotary Club Christmas party. Now it probably was a mistake for the Cape Girardeau Rotary Club to hire Woody. After all, the Cape Rotary Club was like many Rotary clubs: old and conservative.

While the Crackle seated over 300 for dinner and dancing, it had a very low ceiling for the size of the room.

Imagine The Herd with four screeching trumpets, four belching trombones, five soaring saxophones, and a driving, pounding rhythm section. They rocked the joint. It was thunderous!

At one of the intermissions late in the evening, I happened to be standing by the owner of the Crackle, Bud Pearce, as he went up to Woody and proclaimed, "Woody, I've had a bunch of complaints. Your music is too loud; you need to tone it down a bit."

With that Woody shot back, "Who in the hell are you to tell me how to play?"

Bud calmly stated, "Well, as a matter of fact, Woody, I'm the guy who is going to write you your check for tonight's performance."

Uncharacteristically, Woody replied, "In that case, you're right. We're probably a little too loud. We'll tone it down."

Harry James

My 15 minutes of fame almost came during the summer of 1959 at the age of 16. I was at the Colony Club listening to Harry James before my senior year in high school. Harry's band, like Woody Herman's and others of the day, had 16 to 18 players; they weren't called Big Bands for nothing. When there are that many professionals playing at the same time, they can scare you to death.

During one of the intermissions, the band manager came up to me and asked if I played trumpet. Obviously, someone in the room had directed him to me. I think it was my buddy, Bob Sisco. I responded in the affirmative, and he commanded me to follow him.

We went out in the cornfield behind the club, and he handed me a trumpet and said, "Show me your stuff." The Sisco dance band was busy playing throughout Southeast Missouri and Southern Illinois, and I was also a member of the Cape Girardeau Municipal Band that rehearsed on Monday nights and presented concerts on Wednesday nights throughout the summer, so I was in good shape. I played a few licks for him and then he asked if I could play a high "C." I smoothly ran a scale up to the high note and held it for a moment. He then asked me if I could read—a phrase which denotes one's ability to sight-read music. I assured him I could, and he surprised me by offering me a job with the band. The fourth trumpet player was quitting that night. He told me not to tell Harry (as if I would talk to Harry), and they were leaving at noon the next day for Dayton, Ohio.

"If you want the job, get on the bus at the Marquette Hotel at noon," he ordered.

I went home and woke Mom and Dad (the Mayor) about 2:00 a.m. I informed them I was going on the road with Harry James.

Dad looked up and sleepily asked, "What did you say?"

I repeated, "I said, I'm going on the road with Harry James; *we* leave tomorrow at noon from the Marquette!"

"You're not going anywhere until you finish high school *and* college. Get your ass back to your room and go to bed!"

That was the beginning and ending of my real, big-time, professional music career.

A Real Trooper

Back in the '40s, before air-conditioning, inside dances were rather uncomfortable. You would open all the windows, turn on electric fans, and sweat it out. Those were some of the "good old days" people used to hear their parents and grandparents talk about.

On this particular hot summer's night, the Cape Girardeau Country Club, overlooking the Mississippi River, threw a big dance. It was hot. The band was hotter: the Blue Rhythm Boys, the most popular swing band in the area. There was a big crowd, and everyone was having, as they say, "A hot time in the old town tonight!"

Around midnight, the band wailed, "When the Saints Go Marching In." Most all members took solos, so the drummer took a turn. He had assembled his drums in front of a window in an attempt to keep cool. As he beat the drums and crashed the cymbals in what was undoubtedly one of his finest solos, he got to rocking back and forth so much, he fell out of the window backwards.

The newspaper account the next week informed the public that he broke his collarbone on that immortal story and one-half fall. What it didn't report was, as he fell out the window, being a real trooper, he hollered, "Take it away, saxes!"

Sonny & Cher

When Bob Sisco left for California in 1960, he continued writing arrangements for my dance orchestra until his
untimely death in a car accident in 1975. I use many of his
arrangements today; they are still fresh and relevant.

When the Twist craze hit the country, Si Zenter's Big
Band had an instrumental (Twist) version of "Up The
Lazy River." It hit the top of the charts. Along with Jimmy
Dorsey's "So Rare," it's one of the few times an instrumental
recording went to number one on the Top 40. Bob tapped
into the craze and sent me a Twist arrangement of "Jingle
Bells." We play it at Christmas dances, and it continues to
be a big hit for us.

Sonny & Cher opened each TV show with a big produc-
tion number. At the end, they would break for a commercial
and come back with a reprise of that opening number.

I was sitting in front of the TV, watching their Christmas
special one year. To my surprise, the introduction of our arrangement of "Jingle Bells" that Bob had sent me a couple
of years earlier started playing. As I jumped up, the phone
rang. It was my brother Don, yelling, "They're playing our
chart!" Sure enough, Bob's name was listed as an arranger
on the credits at the end of the show.

Jack Stalcup

Jack Stalcup had a Midwest territorial orchestra for over four decades. It was a tenor band, meaning the musical arrangements featured the tenor saxophone as the lead sax rather than an alto sax. The rhythm consisted mostly of two-beats to the measure. In other words, it was square by most of today's musical standards in sound and rhythm. While swing is four-beats to the measure and exudes a more rhythmic pulse, the two-beat style was popular in the '20s, '30s, and early '40s. As a result, Jack was stuck in the '30s.[*]

Jack had a good personality and sold his band well; so well, he made his living doing it. That's quite a feat in small-town U.S.A. He even had a couple of his recordings make the charts in the '40s. He played at the Purple Crackle Club in East Cape Girardeau, Illinois, every Sunday night for over 20 years.

Jack was notorious for being forgetful, especially on the bandstand. He probably was nervous when performing, and it sometimes created funny situations, as it did one night at the Roseland Ballroom in New York City. It had taken him several years to finally get to that famous big-band venue.

---

[*] Now that's the pot calling the kettle black, because I'm kind of stuck in the '40s. I, too, have an orchestra that performs in a six-state area. I've been performing for five decades. I came along 15 to 20 years after Jack when the big swing bands were beginning to fade. However, when I play Woody Herman's "Woodchopper's Ball" or Artie Shaw's "Night & Day" or Les Brown's "I've Got My Love To Keep Me Warm" or Tommy Dorsey's great theme song "I'm Getting Sentimental Over You" or the alma mater of the big band era, Glenn Miller's "In The Mood," can you blame me?

In those days, there were always 300 to 400 dancers at the venue and several hundred thousand people listening to the live radio broadcast throughout the five boroughs that make up New York City.

He was understandably nervous, and, at one point during the live radio broadcast, asked everyone to come onto the floor and dance to a beautiful arrangement of his waltz medley "It Was Fascination" and "Try To Remember." After he announced "It Was Fascination," in his nervousness, he had a mental block and stuttered, "And, and, and. . ." and he forgot the name of the second song.

He turned to his band manager, and closest ally, Winston, and whispered rather loudly into the microphone, "Winston, what's the name of the other song?"

Winston immediately replied, "'Try To Remember'."

Jack quickly chirped back into the microphone, "Damn it, Winston, this is no time to be funny. What's the name of the other song?"

All-Night Parties

There was a union of two family fortunes that produced one of Cape's premier couples. The groom was from a pioneer family who made fortunes in manufacturing and stone quarries. His bride was a daughter of the founder one of the nation's largest construction companies, with projects worldwide. I got a call from them in the early '60s saying they wanted me to provide classy music for a house party they were throwing for many of their friends and customers from around the country.

They wanted the music to start at 6:00 p.m. sharp, out under the four-car carport as guests arrived. They planned to eat around 7:00 p.m. and dance until midnight. (This is where I first met Becky Sharp from New Madrid. She was just starting out on what later would become the region's foremost catering service.) So everything began as planned.

It was a beautiful evening. Guests arrived in the wooded grounds to the sounds of our gentle-jazz around 6:00 p.m. The party featured an eclectic gathering of people from all over the country. Then at midnight, *they decided to eat*. We continued playing until 6:00 a.m. That's right, 6:00 a.m.! That was the first of six annual parties with the same 12-hour format.

In those days Cape Girardeau had three radio stations: KFVS, the old-timers' station; KGMO, the rock station; and KZIM, the country station. KZIM was the flagship radio station that would launch the Zimmer family into a major radio and telecommunications conglomerate in our region. KFVS radio carried St. Louis Cardinals baseball games and remained on the air until midnight. They usually hired college students to take the late shift on the board.

One morning around 4:30 a.m., one such college kid, Bob Spicer, came walking up the driveway at one of those parties. In surprise I asked, "Spicer, what are you doing here?"

He answered, "Well, Digger, I signed off at midnight and went over to the Crackle. Then I made my way to the Colony Club, Dawn Club, and the Little Villa. At that point, it was time to go home. I got out of my car up on Perry Avenue across from the Catholic Cemetery, and I swear to God, I heard a trumpet playing 'Mack the Knife!' I told myself, Spicer, you're drunk, you can't be hearing 'Mack the Knife' at 4:30 a.m. I listened again in that quiet time of morning, and sure enough, I heard a trumpet playing 'Mack the Knife!' I got in my car, rolled the window down, and followed the music. So here I am! Where's the bar?"

III

Tammany Hall

Politicians

While there is much controversy in today's political arena with one-issue groups and the polarization that accompanies them, primarily fueled by talk radio and 24-hour TV news channels, public service is still a high and noble profession. The quality of our lives depends, to a great degree, on the quality of the people we elect to public office.

My family has been steeped in politics for as long as I can remember. My grandfather, J. Frank Masterson, served one four-year term as Cape County Treasurer. Dad ran an unsuccessful campaign for Cape County Sheriff, later served many years as mayor of Cape, and was a judge on the Cape Girardeau County Court at the time of his death at the age of 58 in 1968. My older brother, Walter Joe, served two terms as Cape County Coroner. I served two terms on the Cape Girardeau Board of Education, serving one as president. I then served in the Missouri House of Representatives for two terms (4 years) and made an unsuccessful bid for the United States Congress in 1982.

Some pundits say, "Politics makes strange bedfellows." Many times that's true. However, politics can be a unifying force for good, especially when partisanship is set asisde. Today's political acrimony seems especially brutal. Going back a generation or two, it wasn't always that way here in Cape. There were three families prominent in politics: the Rusts, Limbaughs, and Fords. The Rusts and Limbaughs were Republicans, while we Fords were Democrats. We were on opposite sides of the political spectrum, but we respected each other, worked for the common good, and remained friends. One of the bonds between us was Centenary United Methodist Church: we worshiped together every Sunday. Athletics was another bond (American Legion Baseball) and, to complete the triad, public service.

The Rusts

One would be hard pressed to find a more self-made person than Wayne Rust. As a young man during the Great Depression, he along with members of his family left Rector, Arkansas, for better employment in Detroit, Michigan. He had numerous jobs and finally landed in an upholstery shop.

Poor and struggling to make ends meet, he and a friend, Bud Martin, and their wives made the bold move to go into business, relocating in Cape Girardeau just a few miles from Mrs. Rust's home of Bell City, Missouri. Wayne said on many occasions, "All we had between us was a 50 pound bag of beans when we arrived in Cape."

Over the years, they built a multi-state furniture dynasty: Rust & Martin Furniture Store. After Mr. Martin's untimely death in an automobile accident, the Rust family purchased Martin's interest. It became the largest furniture operation between St. Louis and Memphis, catering to the carriage trade. Just like our funeral home, the whole family pitched in: Wayne's wife Eva, and sons Harry, Gary, and James.

Each of the sons has been successful: Harry stayed at the store; his sons Steve, David, and Mike worked alongside him expanding the family business; Gary went into politics. After his unsuccessful run for our Eighth District U.S. Congressional seat, he served three terms in the Missouri House of Representatives. Gary built a multi-state newspaper group which has changed the landscape of politics in our region from conservative Democrat to

Republican. He and his sons Gary II, Jon, and Rex own 18 daily and 30 weekly newspapers in eight states (and counting) with over 1,000 employees. The youngest son, Jim, founded RM-COCO, a national wholesale distributor of fabric and window treatments. RM-COCO does business in all 50 states, several foreign countries, and employs 115 people.

National Champs—Almost

Wayne Rust and Dad had spirited political discussions over the years. They generally set them aside on the many American Legion baseball trips we took for several summers in the early '50s on our quest to be national champion. We almost made it. Wayne had this habit of driving with his head turned to the back seat as he talked. It seemed like he never looked at the road. Before interstate highways, he scared us to death on those old two-lane hilly roads.

Dad swore that the Rust & Martin dynasty got its roots in Altus, Oklahoma, in 1952. We were there for the national sectional tournament. The Altus Legion team was touted to be national champions because they had the two most celebrated pitchers in the Midwest: the brothers Von and Lindy McDaniel of later St. Louis Cardinals fame. Well, they hadn't heard of Cape's team. We knocked both of them out of the box and headed the next week to the super sectional in Bloomington, Illinois—the last stop before the Final Four.

During the tournament in Altus, Wayne got on a betting roll. When Don Koch would come to the plate, he'd bet one of those Oklahoma wheat farmers $20 that Don would get a double, and Don would. He would predict Dub Suedekum would hit a homer, and Dub would also deliver. He would cash in when his son Gary and Paul Stehr would turn a double play. Dad said it was uncanny: "Wayne could do no wrong."

I learned of this on the way home because I was busy with my duties as the batboy. Wayne predicted double plays, walks, steals, etc., and hardly ever missed. Dad claimed Wayne busted the wheat farmers and left Oklahoma with a wad of bills that would choke a horse! Dad told this story many times at The Grove. He went to his grave insisting (tongue in cheek) the episode put Rust & Martin in the black.

We lost the championship of the next tournament in the last inning on a ground ball that trickled between our left fielder's legs. The team that beat us, Cincinnati, went on to the Final Four and won the national championship. No team in the Final Four came within ten runs of Cincinnati. We had the better team.

The catcher on that team, Russ Nixon, won the national batting crown with a batting average of .395, even though Walter Joe led the nation with an average of .548 in national tournament play. However, one had to be in the Final Four to qualify. Nixon went on to play and manage in the major leagues. Walter Joe and several others on our team starred in college or played professional baseball.

The Limbaughs

Rush Limbaugh, Sr., the patriarch of Cape's First Family, was a distinguished lawyer for many decades. He was the oldest practicing attorney in the country at the time of his death in 1996 at the age of 104. He served in the Missouri Legislature and was president of the Missouri Bar Association. Two of his sons, Rush Jr. and Stephen, followed him into law. They had distinguished careers. Ronald Reagan named Stephen a federal district judge in St. Louis. Stephen Jr., an attorney, circuit judge, and, like his father, a former Cape Girardeau County Prosecutor, was a member of the Missouri Supreme Court. He served one term as Chief Justice and is currently a U.S. District Court judge.

On occasion, Mr. Limbaugh, Sr., and I would compare our service in the Missouri Legislature, his in the early '30s, and mine in the late '70s, and early '80s. Those conversations produced the notion that the issues and dynamics of crafting legislation really never changed much—just different faces.

In December 2007, it was announced that Stephen Jr. was nominated and in 2008 was confirmed for a federal judgeship for the Eastern District of Missouri by President George W. Bush. He follows his father in that position and sits on the bench in the new federal courthouse in Cape Girardeau named for his grandfather, Rush Hudson Limbaugh, Sr. Two of Rush Junior's sons are nationally known—Rush III, known in his childhood as Rusty—the radio personality, and David, attorney, syndicated columnist, and author.

That Damn Rush Limbaugh

Dad and Rush Jr. were great friends. While on the op-posite sides of the political spectrum, they had a healthy re-spect for one another. Rush Jr. was a fighter pilot in WWII, and aviation was his true love. Throughout his many years as Mayor of Cape Girardeau, Dad always appointed Rush to the Municipal Airport Board. He knew Rush was knowl-edgeable, interested, and would always devote whatever time necessary to do the job.

One evening in 1950, Dad came home from his office in the Common Pleas Court House madder than a hornet. "That Damn Rush Limbaugh," he groaned. "What's wrong?" I inquired. "I kicked him out of my office this afternoon," he replied. "You did what?" I asked. "I kicked him out of my office today," he repeated. "Why did you do that?" I queried. "Because he was bad-mouthing Harry Truman, that's why. I told him if he continued criticizing my President, to get the hell out of my office!"

In 1960, Dad came home from the office one day shak-ing his head, laughing almost uncontrollably. "That damn Rush Limbaugh, that *damn* Rush Limbaugh," he kept say-ing. "I never thought I'd hear it. I *never* thought he'd admit it," Dad continued laughing.

"What are you talking about? I thought you kicked him out of your office," I reminded him. "Oh no, that was years ago," he answered. "So what went on?" I asked.

Dad replied, "Well, he was in the office this afternoon and he finally proclaimed, 'Doc, I hate to admit it, but that damn Harry Truman was a great one!'"

For Dad, to get Rush Limbaugh to say anything good about a Democrat was, for him, like winning a state championship in baseball or basketball.

We loved Harry Truman.

Dad and Rush Jr. traveled together on many occasions to Washington D.C. to obtain grants for runway extensions and other infrastructure improvements, as they developed the Cape airport into a regional hub. It would have been fun eavesdropping on their political bantering during those trips to the real seat of power.

Ford Mustang

The Ford Motor Car Company missed their "Ad of the Century." Rush Limbaugh, Jr. (father of Rush and David), weighed over 300 pounds. His voice possessed a deep, resonant tone. When he spoke, everybody listened. He made a mighty presence in the courtroom. He too had inherited the eloquence of his father. His wife Millie's physique was the antithesis of her husband's: thin and nearly six feet tall. She was about as sweet a person as you would ever want to meet. She always greeted you with a great big smile.

She was also a cut-up, funny, and talented, a comedic singer in the genre of Carol Burnett. I collaborated with Millie and Mary Frances Kinder, mother of our Missouri Lieutenant Governor, Peter Kinder, as they teamed up and stole the show in our local Jaycee Follies year after year. My combo provided the music for all those shows—almost 20 years.

So there they were—a man of over 300 pounds, and a thin, six-foot woman, and for a period of time, they drove a Ford Mustang convertible. Seeing them get into that Mustang was a sight to behold, and I laughed every time I saw it. I could see a Ford Mustang television commercial in the making. If Rush Jr. and Millie could get in and out of a Ford Mustang, anyone could.

Ford Motor Company would have sold thousands more.

Court of Appeals

One of my favorite recollections of Mr. Limbaugh, Sr., occurred the day Circuit Judge Stan Grimm was sworn into the Missouri Court of Appeals at Courthouse Park in Cape. Stan was an outstanding lawyer, circuit judge, and Democrat. It was a hot, sweltering, summer day. Not much of a breeze. The park houses the Court of Common Pleas, one of only two such courts in Missouri. The building is a stately brick, white-columned building situated high above the Mississippi River.

All the finest barristers from Southeast Missouri and St. Louis were present, including the current Court of Appeals judges. It was a grand sight. Egos were outweighed only by the old, magnificent trees and other beautiful surroundings of nature at that impressive spot. Most dignitaries had removed their suitcoats and loosened their ties. Not Mr. Limbaugh. He was always dressed in his ever-present vested, conservative, pin-striped suit.

As side conversations continued before the formal swearing-in, I heard several out-of-town attorneys asking each other, "Who is this old man who is to give the keynote speech?" They had never heard of him and looked with a hint of disdain at the old man who was going to take up valuable time on such a hot, miserably humid day.

People who think the current Rush Limbaugh is an orator never heard his grandfather, or for that matter, his father. The elder Limbaugh was the master. He stood above the crowd in the old bandstand and proceeded to wow the audience with a complete history of the Missouri Court of

Appeals—without notes. I never saw him use notes in all the times I heard him speak.

FDR & Harry

We are generally the product of our environment. It's no different with our political philosophy. We form many of our political values from our family: father, mother, even grandparents. I've always gotten a kick out of Republican friends who say, "You're a Democrat because your dad was." To a large degree, they're correct. In my case, it started with both sets of grandparents, especially with Dad's father, Dr. W.W. Ford.

Grandpa had the large classic picture of Franklin Delano Roosevelt, with his top hat, cape, and cigarette in a long holder, hanging in his reception office. Dad said the aristocratic picture of him used to infuriate Republicans. When Missouri's finest, Harry Truman, was elected president, Grandpa hung a large picture of Harry right beside FDR. My father, mayor of Cape most of the years between 1948 and 1964, would chastise him for hanging them there where all his Republican patients would have to practically stumble over them to get in the door. Grandpa would only scoff and say, "They are great Americans, and my patients should admire and respect them."

Grandpa's response reminded me of Harry Truman taking one of his famous early walks. A television reporter accompanying him one morning asked him if it was true he had never split his ticket. He responded. "Yes, that's true."

The reporter then asked, "Mr. President, you've been quoted as saying you always vote for the best man."

Truman responded, "That's right, turn here," as he motioned the reporter to turn the corner with him.

"How is that possible, when you say you vote for the best man, but you've never split your ticket?" the reporter quizzed.

"That's easy," Truman concluded. "The Democrats always have the best man!"

Grandpa loved Harry Truman.

With that kind of lineage it would have been tough being anything but a Democrat in the Ford household.

Walter Joe's First Vote

Grandpa never remarried after Grandma died of pneumonia in 1943. He drove in from Gordonville and attended Centenary United Methodist Church with us every other Sunday. He would eat noon dinner at our house, spend time chatting, and return to Gordonville late in the afternoon. On the other Sundays, he would repeat the process with my Aunt Neva and Uncle Elmore at the First Presbyterian Church, even though he was a member of Centenary. Dad and Grandpa both smoked cigars, so after dinner, they would smoke those cigars all afternoon in the living room, driving my mother crazy. In the winter, you could cut through the smoke with a knife.

After November of 1949, when Dad opened the funeral home, he would sit under the trees at The Grove in his tie, with the sleeves of his white shirt rolled up, a cigar in his mouth, waiting for the phone to ring (it seldom did) with his buddies around him, solving the problems of our city, state, and nation. One of the reasons Mom didn't mind The Grove: it got Dad's cigars out of the house.

On Sundays, Mom always cooked a beef roast with potatoes, carrots, and onions—that way, dinner was ready when we returned from church. With our Democratic views (spawned by Grandpa), one would think the table discussions would go smoothly most of the time. On this particular Sunday, it didn't work out that way.

Walter Joe had just turned 21 and mentioned he voted for Sis Stehr for Clerk of the Circuit Court. Mrs. Stehr was the mother of Paul Stehr. Paul, Walter Joe, Gary Rust, Don

Koch, Dub Suedekum, Jim Welter, Joe Weaver, Truman Blackman, and John Moll, to name a few, grew up playing baseball together. They were like part of the family. They won the State American Legion Baseball Tournament twice, went on to win sectionals, and, one year, they were one out from going to the national Final Four. I was the batboy.

When Walter Joe proudly announced that he had voted for Mrs. Stehr, Grandpa looked up from the table, and in a stern, inquisitive inflection inquired, "What did you say, boy?"

Walter Joe responded, "I voted for Sis Stehr."

Grandpa sternly replied, "We don't do that around here."

"But Grandpa," Walter Joe pleaded, "she's Paul's mother. She's widowed, and she's unopposed!"

"That doesn't make any difference," he shot back. "We must stay loyal to the Democratic Party!"

We never again mentioned voting for Republicans in Grandpa's presence.

Hit the Road

Jack was Tuck's oldest son. (Remember Tuck's funeral?) He, too, was quite a character—a chip off the old block. He was short, stocky, and strong—like a pit bull. One wouldn't want to mess with him. He was a quintessential bartender: smart, with a quick wit and good sense of humor. He tended bar at Les Seabaugh's Blue Note on Broadway for many years.

I hadn't seen Jack in a while until I ran into him in St. Louis. His buddy Donk had opened a classy bar, called "The Bulls and Bears," in downtown St. Louis on the same block as the Adams Mark Hotel, now the Hyatt Regency. I heard about it and stopped in one day when I was up there on business. To my surprise, there was Jack behind the bar.

I ordered their specialty drink, a Bloody Bull, a Bloody Mary made with beef bouillion. They were one of the first watering holes to make such a drink in our area. We began talking, and I asked in amazement why he was up there in St. Louis after all those years in Cape.

He answered, "Jerry, one day a bunch of my buddies at the Blue Note convinced me I should run against your Dad for Mayor. I knew I couldn't beat him, but after a few drinks, they talked me into it. They collected the $50 filing fee and drove me to City Hall to file. As you may remember, I only got 18 votes. I figured as long as I had lived in Cape, and only got 18 votes, it was time to buy a gun and get out of town!"

Bingham Sketches

Governor Kit Bond and his wife Carolyn toured Missouri in 1976 raising money to save 112 George Caleb Bingham sketches of *River Life* from leaving our state; the sketches were important works by the famous Missouri painter. Mercantile Library in St. Louis had possession of the valuable works of art and was planning to auction them to the highest bidder. A reception was held at Southeast Missouri State University in Cape to raise money for the project. Walter Joe and his wife Iris (her nickname is Flower) attended, so I worked the evening visitation at the funeral home. The art event was one of several sponsored by Governor Bond as he successfully raised $300,000 toward the goal of $1.8 million to retain the sketches. Eight hang in the Senate Bingham Gallery in the Capitol, and the others are split between the St. Louis City Art Museum and the Nelson Gallery in Kansas City.

After closing for the evening around 9:30 p.m., I proceeded to the Royal N'Orleans Restaurant for a nightcap. As I approached the restaurant, I noticed a lot of activity. Upon entering the Bistro side of the establishment, I saw Tom Taylor, a highway patrolman originally from Cape, sitting at a table. He was on the governor's detail, his body guard. He informed me the governor and his entourage were in the dining room having a late dinner. We exchanged pleasantries, and I took a seat at the bistro bar.

A few minutes later, out of nowhere, my buddy Skitch Watson appeared. He wanted to know what was going on.

When I informed him the governor was in the dining room having a late dinner, he said, "Let's go talk to him!"

I replied, "No way! We're not going to disturb him or his guests."

Skitch replied sternly, "It's okay, I know him. In fact, we're close personal friends."

I've been around the block enough times to know that lots of regular people "claim" to know celebrities, to be their "close personal friends." And yet, Skitch seemed so full of conviction. He stood firm in his assertion; by golly, he knows the governor! I just had never heard Skitch talk about it before, so I said, emphatically, "NO! Skitch take a seat, we don't want to interfere with his evening." With that, he reluctantly went over to the piano bar and ordered a drink.

A few minutes later, Governor Bond and his entourage came around the corner to leave through the bistro exit. Skitch immediately jumped up, went directly to him, grabbed his hand, and shook it vigorously exclaiming, "Governor, Governor, good to see you, good to see you: Skitch Watson here, Skitch Watson. Don't you remember me?" The Governor looked at him with a blank stare that showed everyone in the room he had no idea who this intruder was. Skitch informed, "I met you one time at the Shawneetown picnic!" Needless to say, they didn't hang out at the bar together for a nightcap.

The Circus

In the middle '70s, I was president of the Cape Girardeau Board of Education. We passed a $2.5 million bond issue for additional facilities. Board secretary Hal Lehman and I traveled four hours to the state capitol in Jefferson City, received the negotiable bearer bonds, and delivered them the next day to the purchaser, Mercantile Bank in St. Louis.

At the conclusion of the task, we were taken to the Noonday Club atop one of the downtown skyscrapers for lunch. One can imagine the scene: glass walls, great view, old money, pin-striped suits, grey hair, no women, nobody under 65 years of age, and quiet—real quiet. Solemn would be a better description.

When we entered to sit with the judge, who was the principal of the law firm engaged by Mercantile to oversee the transaction, everyone turned and looked at us (me). I knew I made a mistake not checking what my first wife had packed for me to wear that morning, but, stuck at the motel in Jefferson City without wardrobe options, when I opened my hanging bag, I reluctantly had to dress for the day.

Visualize the scene as I walked into the Noonday Club. Remember, it was the early '70s, and leisure suits were the style. I was wearing blue and white, small-checked, double-knit, bell-bottomed trousers; a blue, double-knit shirt; a red, white, and blue double-knit tie; maroon, heeled, patent leather boots; and a double-knit, blue sport coat with white piping along the edges. I glowed! To them, in their conservative space, I'm sure I looked like a flashing neon sign.

We finished lunch around 2:00 p.m. Most of the gentlemen had left, when a little, old, crusty man sauntered up and inquired, "Judge, how are you, Judge?"

The judge answered, "I'm okay, how are you? I haven't seen you lately."

The old man said he'd just returned from his ninth African safari with Marlin. (Marlin Perkins of Mutual of Omaha TV fame had been curator of the world-acclaimed St. Louis Zoo for many years.) "This time it was a photo safari. We just took pictures," the old man continued.

The judge then pronounced, "We have people in town doing some bonding business."

With that, the old man slowly looked me up and down and said, "Oh yes, I see. I wondered what time the circus came to town."

Well, my immediate thought was to hit the old bastard. Then I broke out laughing as did the rest. I deserved every bit of what he dished out and more. Some wives shouldn't dress men for business.

The Laundry Room

Every American should participate in our democracy by running for elective office, especially local city council or school board. My two terms on the Cape Girardeau Board of Education were the four toughest, but most rewarding, years of my short public career. When close to the people, one has to justify his or her actions to neighbors every day, face-to-face. The same can be said of city issues—they're immediate and personal. The rewards, however, are also immediate and personal. One can see the results in a smile, a word, a handshake, or gleam of approval.

Jefferson City is a four-hour drive from Cape Girardeau. Issues are of a broader nature, affecting people, businesses, and organizations in a more general way. Most people learn of your legislative actions in newspapers after the fact. As a result, the House of Representatives was a piece of cake compared to serving as a local elected official.

When I was elected to the Missouri House of Representatives in 1978, Renz Farm was the Missouri prison for women. It was located immediately across the Missouri River bottoms from the Capitol in Jefferson City. Newly elected Missouri Representatives and Senators visited it on the bi-annual Freshman Tour, a three-week trip across Missouri, designed to acquaint new members of the General Assembly with the enormity and complexity of state government: budget, economy, regions, services, universities, community colleges, prisons, mental health facilities, etc.

Approximately 70% of the nearly 7,000 women incarcerated in Missouri are there for nonviolent drug offenses. The women I talked to in the laundry room of Renz Farm were there for more serious crimes.

Our group of thirty-four had been there for about an hour when I wandered off from the group and accidentally stumbled into the laundry room. I struck up a fascinating conversation with five or six female inmates—so fascinating that I lost track of time. The legislative group left the premises on the bus. Upon discovering that I wasn't aboard, and also not in the lead Highway Patrol car with Sergeant Joe Dayringer, they returned to rescue me.

Oblivious to the outside world, I was inquiring into the criminal activity that placed the women in prison. One of them replied, "I shot my husband."

"You shot your husband?" I responded in surprise.

"Yes, I shot him," she reaffirmed.

"How did you do *that*?" I grimaced.

"I shot him in the face with a shotgun," she replied.

Almost in fright, I shouted, "Why did you do that?"

With no remorse she proudly proclaimed, "Because the no-good, dirty, rotten, son-of-a-bitch deserved it, that's why!"

With that, I was escorted out of the laundry room and onto the bus.

Inauguration Night

In January of 1979, after completion of the Freshman Tour, it was time for our inauguration in the Capitol at Jefferson City, Missouri. About forty family members and friends from Cape Girardeau, including Skitch Watson and his wife, attended the ceremony. All the elected officials—members of the House, Senate, Executive Branch, Supreme Court, and U.S. Congress—assembled in the Governor's Oval Office for the grand march down the Grand Staircase in the Rotunda to the pleasure of 5,000 guests and state-wide media. As one can imagine, the office was crowded shoulder-to-shoulder. The Adjutant General's Staff guarded the door. No one was admitted that wasn't supposed to be there—no one except my buddy Skitch and his wife. How they got in is anybody's guess. Maybe he was *now* friends with the Governor?

We were all there in our tuxedos and gowns, and Skitch in his suit, anxiously awaiting the sound of the trumpet, when all of a sudden, Skitch shouted at the top of his lungs, "Senator Murray, Senator Murray!" Everyone stopped their individual conversations and directed their attention to Skitch. Skitch ran over to him, grabbed his hand, shook it violently, and acknowledged, "Senator, Senator Murray," as the elder Senator sat quietly on a small couch in the middle of the room with his grey-haired wife in her beautiful beaded gown.

"Skitch, Senator. Skitch Watson! You remember me."

The Senator sat there completely baffled by this trespasser. It was obvious to everyone in the room he had no idea who was addressing him, just like Governor Bond had responded several years earlier at the Royal N'Orleans restaurant.

"Don't you remember, Senator? We got drunk together one night at the Chester (Illinois) Elks Club!"

A few minutes later, Skitch's wife went over to the immense walnut desk and inquired, "Is this really the Governor's desk?"

Skitch answered, "Why, yes, honey."

With everyone in the room looking on again, he immediately sat her in the Governor's chair and twirled her around several times, as she proclaimed in a high-pitched voice, "Oooh, Skitch just knows everybody!"

Let Him Die

In days gone by, before the partisan bickering that dominates current political discourse, the Missouri Legislature was, at times, a social club. While issues and political differences were important, to be sure, there was a certain camaraderie that permeated the air. We fought by day and partied by night. As a result, compromise and consensus were generally the order of the day.

One evening in April of 1980, legislators from both sides of the aisle were socializing at Rip's Mor-E-O Lodge on the Moreau River at the eastern edge of Jefferson City. The food was tasty, the St. Louis police officers' rock-n-roll band was great, and everyone was having a good time. One Senator was having an exceptionally good time.

John Schneider (D), St. Louis County, was a young lion of the Senate, serving as Majority Floor Leader. Before term limits, the Senate was known as a great deliberative body with members possessing a breadth of knowledge amassed by many years of experience: Richard Webster (R), Carthage; Paul Bradshaw (R), Springfield; and Emory Melton (R), Cassville, were outstanding orators. John Russell (R), Lebanon; Norman Merrell (D), Monticello; John Scott (D), St. Louis City; Harold Caskey (D), Butler; and Jim Mathewson (D), Sedalia, were master crafters of legislation. And even my buddy, Danny Staples (D), Eminence, could occasionally keep up with the big boys with his quick mind and down-home humor.

Well, John Schneider left the party shortly before Representative W.T. Dawson, my longtime friend, Calvin Wells, who was a lobbyist at the time for Missouri Utilities head-quartered in Cape Girardeau, and I. As we drove toward our apartment, we saw headlights bobbing up and down out in the front of us at the side of the highway. "My God, I think someone just flipped a car," exclaimed W.T.

We sped to the spot, scrambled down the embankment, fought through high weeds and underbrush, and to our surprise found the car turned upside down with the wheels spinning in a cloud of smoke. Dawson and Wells quickly raised the MG convertible a bit while I grabbed the driver's shoulders and pulled him from beneath the car. There to our amazement lay Senator John Schneider. He groaned, "I can't move." Wells climbed back up the ditch and waved several cars down to go for help.

The ambulance finally arrived to transport Schneider to St. Mary's Hospital where he was diagnosed with a broken pelvis, punctured lung, busted spleen, many broken ribs, other complications, and a large bruised ego. He was in the hospital for over a month, and his recovery lasted for several more.

Two weeks after the accident, Dawson, Wells, and I were escorted into the Senate Chamber for a solemn appreciation ceremony for saving the Senator's life. We stood before the Dais as words of appreciation were delivered by several Senators. A few tears were shed as Clarence Hetlin (D), Independence, read and presented us with the impressive, framed Senate Resolutions.

As we turned to leave, Senator Cliffy Jones (R), St. Louis County, a great orator in his own right, whispered into the microphone loudly so everyone could hear, "Why didn't you let the son-of-a-bitch die?"

The galleries immediately erupted with laughter. Over the years, Senators have (in jest, I think) never forgiven us for our heroic gesture.

The Dirty Dozen

Politics is the art of compromise and coalition building. The vast majority of the population in Missouri resides in the two metropolitan areas of Kansas City and St. Louis. For decades the Bootheel,* being solidly Democratic, would hook up with either St. Louis or Kansas City, depending on the subject matter, and control the legislative process in the Capitol at Jefferson City.

The two big cities never got along and still don't. They compete and are jealous of each other. At times, we rural legislators would entice an argument on the floor of the House of Representatives between the two, sit back, and watch the fight for days. We always felt Missourians were safe when that happened, because nothing transpired.

The fight for a new Speaker of the House was a tough one in January of 1981, my second term. Joe Holt, from Fulton, Missouri, was an outstanding Majority Floor

---

* The Bootheel is an area that stretches from Cape Girardeau more than 100 miles south to the Arkansas line. In prehistoric times, the Gulf of Mexico covered the Delta land up to the foot of the Benton, Missouri, hill on I-55 about fifteen miles south of Cape Girardeau. It contained the largest stand of cypress trees on the North American continent. At the beginning of the twentieth century, the Little River Drainage District was constructed to drain the swamp and convert the land into valuable, irrigated farmland. When the rest of the country is in a drought, over three trillion gallons of water are just thirty feet below the surface of the Bootheel. The area is still known as "Swamp-east" Missouri. For more information on the Little River Drainage District, log on to their web site at: www.lrddmo.com. It is one of the only man-made construction projects besides the Great Wall of China that reportedly can be seen with the naked eye from space.

Leader, third in command. In fact, he was the last truly great one. He knew the issues, *read* the bills, and spoke eloquently and passionately for the majority position on almost every piece of legislation debated on the floor of the House. My predecessor, Gary Rust, would have been a great one, but he was in the minority party (Republican) in those days. I saw a lot of Gary Rust in Joe Holt.

Joe lost the Speaker's race, retired from the legislature, and was subsequently elected circuit judge. He lost the Speaker's race because geography played an important role.

Joe was from the center of the state with no real geographic coalition. Kansas City had been out of power in the Rothman years, so they wanted in. They chose the then-Speaker Pro Tempore (second in command) Bob Griffin of Cameron, which is close to Kansas City, as their candidate and enlisted the Bootheel to gain the plurality necessary to win. We won.

The twelve who were the core of the campaign, soon to be known as The Dirty Dozen, divided the Democratic Caucus by geography and lobbied them hard until they had the votes. The Kansas City area members were Gladys Marriott, Leo McKamey, Ronnie DePasco. There was also Stan Thomas, Liberty; Randy Robb, Gladstone; Jim Russell, Savannah; W.T. Dawson, Independence; Jim Riley and Dewey Crump, St. Louis County; Howard Garrett, Jefferson County; and Marvin Proffer and me from Cape Girardeau County.

The other factor in the race was the competition between railroads and big trucks. Speaker Rothman was aligned with the railroads and their lobbyist, John Britton, the Dean of the lobbyist corps. Joe Holt joined that camp. Bob Griffin was aligned with the truckers and their lobbyists, George Burress and Bob Wilson. There were myriads of other dynamics at play as there always are in political dramas, but choosing members from the various regions of the state tipped the balance. Bob Griffin held the Speaker's chair longer than anyone in Missouri history: 17 years.

Getting Even

My close friend and ally, Marvin Proffer, was an integral part of the Dirty Dozen team. Marvin was first elected in 1964 and ultimately served 26 years! At one juncture, he lost a bitter campaign for Speaker of the House. The new Speaker's first order of business when he took office was to strip Marvin of all committee assignments. So when the next race occurred, Marvin and his allies—Griffin and the big truck lobby—were ready. As the previous story related, we won. Marvin served with distinction as the House Budget Chairman for the next eight years.

The first floor of Missouri's impressive Capitol building is reserved for a museum of our state's history. Margaret and I visit the various State Capitols as we travel. There are many outstanding edifices, but none rivals Missouri's, other than our nation's Capitol building in Washington, DC. When the capitol was finished in 1911, there remained a surplus of over $300,000. That surplus was used for murals, statuary, and other aesthetic artifacts. Later came the coup de grace: the Thomas Hart Benton murals in the House of Representatives' third floor lounge, depicting the history of Missouri.

As great as the museum is, the west end alcove never had much of a display. It needed a renovation. The Speaker's wife at the time decided that a small theater dedicated to "How a Bill Becomes a Law" would be appropriate. She further thought that a short film on the subject featuring her husband, the Speaker, would be the perfect pinnacle for the display and his public service.

So the last night of the Legislative Session in 1980, during the 6:00 p.m. to 8:00 p.m. break (we went until midnight in those days), a truckload of flowers was placed all around the dais. At 8:00 p.m. sharp, the Speaker gave a 20-minute dissertation on "How a Bill Becomes a Law," at the expense of legislation waiting to be acted upon. One of my bills, at the top of the list to be debated, was being delayed by the speech.

Now, Marvin Proffer finally got even. His seat on the floor was always at the third row aisle next to the lower gallery. He could easily move around the room without disturbing debate. As the speech began, the TV video crew was filming the event in the lower gallery for the museum theater. Marvin, knowing what was happening, stood immediately in front of the camera. The camera moved, and so did Marvin. They moved again, and so did Marvin. This cat and mouse game continued several times.

The TV crew was stuck because they weren't allowed on the House floor. They were at Marvin's mercy. Marvin ruined the speech. He got even. The video only consisted of the back of Marvin's head! The theatre was never built, the Speaker lost his place in the museum history, and Marvin has lived happily ever after.

Earthquake

Some actors make good politicians; some politicians are good actors. Deciphering the difference can be difficult. Many successful politicians are good, if not great, orators. The ability to craft and present words in an effective, inspiring manner is a linchpin for politicians.

There was an upheaval throughout the state, unequalled since the New Madrid earthquake of 1812, when University of Missouri Chancellor Barbara Uehling and Athletic Director Dave Hart announced a new premium ticket policy for Mizzou football games in 1980. Upgrades to the stadium were needed, and the scheme to raise the money caused great alarm. Long-time boosters were forced to pay huge sums to retain their seats, and in addition, individual ticket prices were raised substantially. The scheme caught everyone off-guard. The tremors of public outcry were unsettling with the faithful fans.

After weeks of futile attempts at compromise, we summoned the Chancellor and the A.D. to Jefferson City. We met in the beautiful, world-acclaimed House of Representatives lounge with Thomas Hart Benton murals depicting the history of Missouri surrounding us on the walls. Each legislator contributed to the inquisition, one by one. It lasted for an hour and a half.

At one point Representative Red Markwell (D), Florissant, stated, "You people come down here from Mizzou, hold out your brown paper bags, and walk away with over $400 million with no accountability. That's going to stop!"

As the inquisition continued, it was obvious to everyone that Dave Hart wanted to fight. He puffed up, frowned, clinched his fists, and didn't hesitate to show his disdain for anyone challenging his authority or his decisions. After all, he was the A.D.! Chancellor Uheling's reaction was decidedly different. She seemed to take the issue to heart. At one point, I think I detected a slight tear in her eye.

Francis "Bud" Barnes (R), Kirkwood, was an eloquent speaker. He represented the people of his district with distinction for many years in the House of Representatives. He was an aristocrat, who always told me he was of the Barnes Hospital family of St. Louis. You could guess his profession at first glance by his appearance: conservative pin-striped suit, grey hair, glasses, bowtie, and pipe.

Bud gave the final summation. In a very slow, legalistic, regal inflection he began:

> I come to you from the days of Paul Chrisman [an All-American from years past]. For decades my constituents have supported the university in the good and lean years. Over time, they have contributed to the School of Agriculture, the School of Engineering, the internationally acclaimed School of Journalism, and, of course, the time-honored School of Law. And my good people of Kirkwood have also contributed their most valuable asset: the children of our community.

He gently rose from his chair and slowly concluded, "I sadly rise today, not to say hello but, unfortunately, to say goodbye."

It was one of his most poignant orations. The room was silent. As he slowly headed toward the massive doors, he tilted his head slightly in our direction and winked. Our entire assemblage arose with heads bowed and somberly left the room, biting our lips to keep from laughing.

Two weeks later, they changed the plan.

Sikeston Farmers

Many visitors come away disillusioned from viewing action on the floor of House and Senate chambers—legislators seem disinterested with the debate taking place. Visitors see empty chairs, members reading, talking among themselves, joking, walking around, leaning against back walls, seemingly oblivious to the discussion and subject at hand. It's reminiscent of the old saying, "The two things one shouldn't watch are the making of laws and sausage!"

While some legislators may be oblivious, most do, in fact, understand the debate. Remember: the bill has probably been around for several years; they may have read the bill in question; may have heard it presented in a committee hearing; most definitely received opinions from people back home through face-to-face contact, phone, fax, or e-mail; held discussions with colleagues who are considered knowledgeable or experts on the subject; and all the while, kept one ear open to any sudden new information from the debate. There really is method to the madness.

Many humorous situations arise in debate in any legislative body on a daily basis. Humor is an essential element of the legislative process. Without it, debate would be even more contentious, and nothing would be accomplished. Some would think that's okay. After all, another axiom is, "We're safe because the legislature is not in Session!"

By way of background to this story, you need to know that many of Missouri's wealthier citizens either have second homes in Florida, or become snowbirds, wintering in

Florida. Depending on the locale, you can drive from Missouri to Florida in one long day.

One day my seatmate, Ozzie Osborne (not the rock star), rose from his chair to promote his license-plate bill for farmers. Ozzie was a big ole boy: 6'4", dark wavy hair, with a classic farmers tan—the red, ruddy complexion with a white forehead shaded from the sun by the bill of a cap. His family farmed over 2,000 acres at Monroe City, up around Hannibal, Missouri—Mark Twain country.

Ozzie started espousing the virtues of his license-plate bill to the assembly when Sikeston* Representative Dennis Ziegenhorn rose and asked the Speaker of the House for permission to inquire of the Gentleman from Monroe.

Ozzie was explaining that state troopers hide behind billboards, large shrubs, and trees at harvest time and unfairly ticket unlicensed farm vehicles that are only used to transport grain to elevators. His bill would have authorized temporary license plates with an 'F' designation to be used only by farmers at harvest time.

Representative Ziegenhorn inquired, "Gentleman, tell me again. What is the purpose of the "F" designation on the license plate?"

Ozzie answered, "So we know who our farmers are."

"Oh, gentleman," Dennis responded, "down where I come from in Sikeston, we know who our farmers are."

"Well, how's that?" Ozzie quizzed.

"Gentleman, we just look for them Mercedes with Florida license plates!" Ziegenhorn exclaimed.

---

* Back in the '50s, Sikeston, a town of 18,000 residents, 30 miles south of Cape Girardeau on Interstate 55, was known in several national publications as the town with the most millionaires per capita in the USA. I don't know how that was established, but there are still many wealthy farmers in that area, and the wealth (thousands of acres of rich Delta farmland) is still held by those families. When you go down the Benton, Missouri, hill about 15 miles south of Cape Girardeau on Interstate 55 to the Delta, row crops of cotton, corn, soybeans, milo, wheat, and now, even rice can be seen for miles and miles.

Law-Abiding Citizen

Senator John Dennis, former First Lady Betty Hearnes, and I rode back and forth to the Capitol most weeks. On this particular Monday, we decided to take the long way around and travel Interstate 70. There is really no good way to get to Jefferson City from the Bootheel. Any way you go, it's a four-hour drive. On this day, I noticed some confusion up ahead, and I accidentally dropped my soda on the floor. As I bent down to pick it up, I reduced my speed.

Upon arrival at my office, my secretary was in a tizzy. "Channel 2 TV from St. Louis is in your office. They want to interview you, but won't disclose the subject matter. I've heard in the halls they are doing some kind of expose about legislators exceeding the speed limit," she exclaimed.

As a freshman legislator, I was a little apprehensive, but I thought, *what the heck; no big deal*. They already had the camera at my desk and initiated the interview with, "Representative Ford, do you believe in abiding by the law?"

Feeling my oats, I answered, "Of course, just like everyone else in this building."

The correspondent continued, "We had a speed trap set up on Interstate 70 today and caught several of your colleagues going well over the 55 mile-an-hour speed limit (the limit at that time). What do you have to say about that?"

I haughtily responded, "I'm shocked."

I'm known to have a heavy foot at times and have received several speeding tickets over the years to prove it. He then said, "Representative Ford, we caught some

156

legislators going over 85 MPH, but out of all of them we caught on camera, you were the only one going 55."

Instinctively, I blurted out laughing, "You gotta be shittin' me!"

Well, my response ended the interview. I didn't make it on the tube that night in St. Louis. And I never told them of my dropping the soda when I saw the commotion of several vans at the side of the road earlier in the day up on I-70, which was obviously where the speed trap had been located.

Governor Joe Teasdale

"Walking Joe" Teasdale from Kansas City began his statewide political career running for the U.S. Senate in 1975. He gained regional attention by walking around the state during his campaign. Inexplicably late in the campaign, right before the filing deadline in 1976, he switched and became a candidate for Governor.

Christopher "Kit" Bond was the incumbent. Kit was young, good looking, and popular. He had served one term as state auditor and was the youngest governor in Missouri history. He was definitely on the move and would not only reclaim his governor's chair after being defeated by Teasdale but would later serve many years, with distinction, in the United States Senate.

Young Joe was also brash and full of vim and vigor. At first, few people gave him a chance. However, Joe kept walking and talking, and the campaign tightened. Bond miscalculated his position in the race because he, like everyone else, thought Joe was a lightweight. To make matters worse, Bond didn't make many television or radio buys. With only two weeks to go, the polls were dead even. Bond rushed to buy TV spots, but they were all gone! Teasdale defeated Christopher Bond in our state's biggest political upset of modern time.

Joe had a habit of clearing his throat when he got nervous. One evening he made an appearance before the House Commerce Committee, of which I was a member, with all the TV, radio, and newspaper personalities, and his entourage present. The cameras were rolling.

Our committee was very attendant to his presentation, and most members took detailed notes. We were the epitome of decorum. Afterwards, a long-time pundit of the Capitol came up and congratulated me and the entire committee for our demeanor, attention, and seriousness with which we approached our responsibilities. He said it was maybe the best committee hearing he'd witnessed in many years. I piously thanked him and then burst his bubble.

I explained to him that we weren't merely paying attention to the substance of the governor's presentation. What he thought he saw was, in reality, the members of the committee protecting their investment. Each of us had thrown five dollars in a pot to see how many times the governor would clear his throat during his testimony. The perceived note-taking was simply everyone tabulating the totals, not writing what he said.

Unfortunately, I didn't win the pot.

Swamp Juice

Gerald Ford was President when I was elected to the Missouri House of Representatives in November of 1978. After the election, I used the slogan "Jerry Ford Loves Democrats" to capitalize on the coincidence of our names and the fact we were of separate political parties. I printed brochures, buttons, yard signs, bumper stickers, etc. It caught on, and we had a great time with it. People still get the connection today.

The two main statewide annual Democratic rallies are Hannibal's Democrat Days and Springfield's Jackson Days. They are weekends of political speeches, banquets, parties, receptions, and general camaraderie. I had a hospitality room with my "Jerry Ford Loves Democrats" theme for four years at both events. It was a big hit. People loved the play on the names of me and the president. The responses were, "Hello, Mr. President," "You should be in the White House," and "How's Betty?"

I served Swamp Juice to those attending. It was what many knew in college as Purple Passion, but with lemonade instead of grape juice to cut the grain alcohol. My colleague W.T. Dawson suggested the substitute. "T," hailing from Harry Truman's hometown of Independence, Missouri, knew a thing or two about political rallies. We knew Harry's favorite drink was bourbon and branch water, but we agreed grain alcohol was more appropriate for these events.

One can imagine the effects of the concoction. Most little ole grey-haired ladies loved it. They couldn't get enough of it! It certainly made the festivities livelier. If someone hadn't

fallen into the swimming pool by 3:00 p.m., we figured we hadn't done our job. People talked about it for years.

Twenty-five years later, I'm a lobbyist in the Capitol in Jefferson City representing families of people with mental retardation statewide. I came out of a meeting in the Jefferson Building across from the Capitol around noon on a pretty, sunny day. There was substantial activity around St. Peter's Catholic Church activities building, the Selinger Culture Center. Upon inquiring, I learned it was Pancake Day. Not having had lunch, I proceeded in, paid my six dollars, received my plate of pancakes and sausage, and was ushered to the next empty seat. A minute or two later, two elderly women were seated across the table from me. I noticed one of the ladies immediately looked at me with a quizzical expression.

She barely sat down when she asked, "I think I know you. What's your name?"

I answered, "Jerry Ford."

She jumped up, pointed a finger at me, laughed, and shouted at the top of her lungs, "Swamp Juice!"

The Echo

Betty Hearnes (Missouri's former first lady) and I served in the Missouri Legislature for a number of years. She worked very hard on my campaign for U.S. Congress. The run for Congress had come about because our twelve-year Democrat incumbent congressman had gotten into a scandal previous to the last election after the filing deadline had passed, and he was defeated by a virtually unknown Republican. I carried the banner for the Democratic Party in the next election cycle. At the end of this particular evening during the campaign, Betty went home to Charleston, Missouri, and told her husband Warren, Missouri's first two-term governor, that in all her years in politics, this unexpected event caused the most mayhem she'd ever remembered.

At one point in the campaign, our state senator John Dennis arranged for me to be the keynote speaker at the annual Chamber of Commerce Man of the Year banquet in a small Bootheel town at its Knights of Columbus gymnasium. There were over 100 people in attendance, with several elderly widows seated close to the head table where I was sitting.

The old KC Hall was a gym with a wood floor and high ceiling. The acoustics weren't the best. The PA system was rather loud, and there was a noticeable echo at times when one spoke through the microphone. The evening started out very well; the conversation and meal were excellent. I was in comfortable Democratic territory. After dinner, the usual acknowledgements and introductions were made, then it was time for the Big Event—the announcement of the Man of the Year.

The Master of Ceremonies reviewed the man's accomplishments and announced the winner—a man fondly known as Ole Barney. Ole Barney slowly strode to the podium to thunderous applause. Remember, it was a loud room.

"Thank you. I really appreciate this award. It means a lot to me. Oh, honey, come on up here, honey," as he motioned for his wife to come forward.

"I guess you all wonder why ole Barney has his suit and tie on, don't you?" as he thumped his chest. "Well, it's because I had a suspicion that ole Barney would win this thing. Come on, honey. That's it, come on up here." He continued motioning to her.

"You know, our town is a great place to raise kids, and we have really appreciated you folks and the church and the whole town."

About this time his wife made it up to the podium. She was a pleasant, middle aged, rather buxom woman. Ole Barney continued, as he picked up the corsage that always accompanied the award: "Yes, ole Barney had a suspicion he was going to win. And it's really important because then I knew I would be able to pin this corsage right here on my wife's TIT! (. . . Tit!! . . . Tit! . . . tit)." The word bounced from wall to wall like a ping-pong ball.

After a moment of stunned silence, while he continued to fiddle with the corsage, the whole place went crazy. I started laughing uncontrollably, until I looked out in the front row and saw all the frowns on those elderly widows' faces. They didn't think it was a damned bit funny. They were visibly upset and glared at everyone and everything.

I attempted to sober up by placing my hand over my mouth to conceal my faux pas as best I could, while I calmed down and concentrated on how I was going to top that in my speech. I didn't.

Ronald Reagan

I gave a lot of speeches to a lot of different groups in the year-and-a-half I campaigned for the Eighth Congressional District Seat in Missouri. On one occasion, I spoke to the Missouri State Labor Council Annual Convention in St. Louis. I was giving Ronald Reagan hell. He was president, and I disagreed with a lot of his policies; so did Labor. Reagan had been a Democrat in the past and even President of the Actors Guild. He turned Republican and had recently shut down the air-traffic controllers during their strike. I was preaching to the choir.

At one point in my presentation, I asked the one thousand assembled to shout in unison, "Ronald Reagan, come down from your mountaintop." To which I would answer with a quiet refrain, "And feed the poor."

Once again the verse, "Ronald Reagan, come down from your mountaintop."

And I would quietly respond, "And educate our youth," and so on.

I did these five or six times and had the place rocking. They were really into it. I urged them on one last time. They were yelling at the top of their lungs, literally taking the roof off the place, "Ronald Reagan, come down from your mountaintop." Just as I was about to give my final impassioned chorus, a voice shouted from the back of the convention hall, "Come down, hell! Tell the no-good, dirty, rotten, son-of-a-bitch to jump!"

I didn't top that one either.

All Down Hill

I campaigned for the Eighth U.S. Congressional seat in 1981 and '82. I enjoyed campaigning, and also had a lot of fun, because there were many humorous events that took place along the campaign trail. I met people in their homes, on street corners, at fairs, picnics, parades, receptions, and various meetings. I learned about their problems, hopes, dreams, and aspirations for themselves and their families. I came to appreciate even more the diversity of our state and the goodness of her people. The experience made me a much wiser and more tolerant person.

It was a tough campaign. I was challenging the incumbent who had all the advantages incumbency provides, including outspending me nearly five to one. The race was close but in the end, I lost.

I turned 40 on Election Day, November 2, 1982, and I thought it was a good omen. I was speaking to over 400 Democrats in the high-school auditorium in Salem, Missouri, a few weeks before the election. Once again, I had the place rocking. Most Democrats didn't like Ronald Reagan all that much. After more than a year on the stump, I could pump out my message of changing policies in Washington, DC pretty well.

Toward the end of the talk I naively announced the good omen: "I will be 40 on Election Day, and we will win because everybody knows that life begins at 40." A clairvoyant lady up in the balcony shouted, "It sure does, honey, all—down—hill!"

Not My Brother!

Dr. Ed Spicer, an African-American Special Assistant to Dr. Bill Stacy, President of Southeast Missouri State University, was a great friend. His big smile was infectious. He was always an ardent supporter of mine, and my congressional race was no different. He had arranged to meet me in back of Academic Hall on the campus at 5:30 a.m. and proceed to the Cotton Bowl Restaurant in Marston, Missouri, to meet the black leaders of the Bootheel for breakfast.

Dawn was approaching. There was a low, eerie haze and visibility was negligible. We chanced upon an 18-wheeler jack-knifed in the middle of Interstate 55 down around Scott City. About 10 minutes later, the red lights of a state trooper's car, augmented by the thick fog, approached with siren blazing. As the trooper walked toward us, I recognized him as the African-American trooper who had given me a ticket two weeks earlier. I started laughing as I recalled the event to Dr. Spicer.

My Dixieland band had performed at a big Democratic rally in New Madrid County,* the hub of Harry Truman's party in the Bootheel. At the conclusion of the event, we sped home to get a college student, who had performed with

* There was a mystique about New Madrid County Democratic politics. J.V. Conrad was the prosecuting attorney of New Madrid County back in the '40s and leader of the Bootheel Democratic Party. He reputedly brokered a back-room deal that placed Harry Truman on the ballot with President Roosevelt at the 1944 Democratic National Convention. Without that deal, Truman would never have been Vice President or President.

us, back to his dorm before it closed. As we climbed the Benton hill, I saw the dreaded red lights in my rearview mirror.

This event happened during the legislative session, and members of the legislature aren't supposed to be given misdemeanor tickets during that period—it's in the statutes. The Jefferson City joke was, if stopped say, "Officer, I was in a hurry to get to the Capitol to vote for that pay raise for the Highway Patrol!" Even though I could have protested, I dutifully took my medicine. I didn't want to cause an incident during my congressional campaign, or any other time for that matter.

Before the African-American trooper reached our car, Ed started laughing, too, and told me of an episode he had with the same trooper. Only the week before, the trooper stopped Ed. As he approached, Ed saw he was black and surmised he would be okay. So he rolled his window down and inquired, "What's happ'nin', Brother?" The officer immediately shot back, "Don't give me any of that *brother* shit; I want to see your license," as he wrote out Ed's ticket.

We both were laughing so hard, we couldn't speak to him him as he walked past to take care of more serious business. We never knew if he recognized either of us. While our breakfast had been delayed, we chronicled another story to be told over and over at The Grove.

The Born Loser

My wife, Margaret, and I met through politics. Senator John Dennis was a mutual friend. He fixed us up on a blind date the last Sunday that Jack Stalcup performed at the Purple Crackle, while I was still in the legislature in 1980. We had dinner with John, his wife, and three other couples. We hit it off immediately; the evening went well. We dated for several years, including the time during the congressional campaign, before we married.

On one occasion during this time, I was in New York on business. I knew the Chicago Cubs were in St. Louis to play the Cardinals, so I called her and arranged for her to meet me in a downtown hotel the next evening so we could take in the ballgame.

I arrived around 6:00 p.m. and asked the desk clerk if there were any messages. She said, "No." I asked for my key, and she informed me she didn't have a reservation in my name. Although I thought it strange, since I had made the reservation the preceding day and could tell by the inflection of her voice that she was the one I made the reservation with, I dutifully took another room.

After dropping my bag in the room, I returned to the lobby to wait for Margaret. She didn't show. It was a beautiful night, and downtown St. Louis was hopping as always when the Cubbies are in town. People from Illinois, Indiana, Arkansas, Tennessee, Kentucky, and parts unknown roll into St. Louis to see the great rivalry. Rest stops on the interstate highways bulge before and after the game. I could hear the roar of the crowd with every pitch as I checked the desk several times; still no message, still no Margaret.

Everyone, except me, was rushing around, laughing, and having a good time. The Lions Club was having their state convention. There were several high-school proms at the hotel. The kids looked great in their formals and tuxedos.

After a couple of hours, I couldn't take it any more, so I went to the bar and had a few drinks; still no Margaret. The bartender even gave me a couple of free drinks as I fumed. After three hours of frustration, and several additional trips to the desk to see if there were any messages, I finally went up to the room to retrieve my bag and begin the 120-mile drive down I-55 to Cape. As I entered the room, the phone rang.

I picked it up, and Margaret asked, "Where have you been?"

I screamed, "Where have I been? Where the hell have you been?"

"In your room," she replied.

"In my room," I yelled, "*I'm* in *my* room!"

She then explained she arrived early, but the desk clerk wouldn't let her in my room. The clerk required her to take a room in her name. She had been there all evening, waiting for me. The same clerk eliminated my reservation and didn't remember when I checked in. Well, I went ballistic. After retrieving Margaret, I ran to the front desk and chewed out the girl, big time.

"You've ruined our evening. The Cardinals are playing the Cubs, and we were stranded here waiting for each other due to your incompetence. Look out the window, the game's over!" I also chewed on the manager and anyone else in earshot.

After I calmed down a little, we decided to drive a few blocks to Laclede's Landing down in the old warehouse district on the Mississippi River's edge to eat. The game had just let out and traffic was horrendous. The Cardinals had won the game. Everyone was out in the streets celebrating the victory. Car horns were honking; traffic was at a standstill. It was a madhouse of revelry.

When we finally made it to the Landing, there were no

parking places. There are many nightclubs, restaurants, and bars in the seven or eight block complex, and it seemed as if the whole capacity crowd from Busch Stadium had gone there to party and to celebrate the big, exciting victory. After circling the cobblestone streets and parking lots four or five times, we dejectedly decided to go back to the hotel and eat at the coffee shop.

Of course, the hotel was also a madhouse with fans celebrating the victory. High-school prom students were everywhere. There was a long, slow line at the coffee shop. Lions Club partiers were sobering up! The restaurant was full. We waited patiently, even though at this point, about a quarter to midnight, it was tough. Just at midnight we got to the hostess station, and she informed us, "We close at 12:00 a.m. I'm sorry, but I can't seat anyone after midnight."

Well, I lost it. I made a fool out of myself again, to no avail. We went back to our room and (the final straw), there was no room service at that late hour. We checked out the next morning; they charged me for the room. I was not a happy camper. I won't tell you what I said to them.

To this day, I've never stayed at one of their hotels, eaten one of their damn TV dinners, or bought anything with their name on it—period!

Clinton/Gore

Fresh from the Democratic National Convention, President Bill Clinton and Vice President Al Gore kicked off the 1996 campaign for their second term with a bus caravan starting in Cape Girardeau. They probably picked Cape since it is the hometown of Rush Limbaugh, and they wanted to rub it in a little. It was also easy access by bus to their home states of Arkansas and Tennessee. Anyway, it was a great day for Cape Girardeau.[*]

Over 20,000 people showed up in Capaha Park to see and hear the Clintons and Gores. That was an astonishing number when one considers that our area has become Republican. The turnout showed us that Clinton was the real deal. My Dixieland Band strolled throughout the park, entertaining for several hours as people lined up for security checks. As soon as the program started, we dashed to Cairo, Illinois (about 30 minutes from Cape), to provide music for the crowd that was gathering there. My music

---

[*] When the advance team contacted me as they made their plans for the presidential visit, I insisted that my brother Don and his wife Carolyn be in the receiving line on the tarmac at the Cape airport that my Dad and Rush, Jr., had been so instrumental in improving years before. Don was dying of cancer, and I knew this would be his only chance to visit a minute or two with President Clinton. There was Don, a mere shadow of himself: slumped shoulders, a cane to assist his balance, sunglasses to hide his sunken eyes as he talked to Bill Clinton, and Don's wife Carolyn, always at his side, talking to Hillary, with Air Force One in the background. It was quite a sight. I swell with pride every time I look at my picture of the event. Grandpa Ford loved Harry Truman, and we love Bill Clinton.

groups have performed in Cairo many times over the years, and the city fathers wanted to put on a good show for the people who were patiently waiting for the President and his entourage.

The platform was in the street, and a crowd of about 6,000 was arriving, including quite an array of political celebrities including: Cairo Mayor Jim Wilson, Illinois State Representatives Jim Rhea and David Phelps, U.S. Representatives Jerry Costello and Paul Simon, Kentucky Governor Paul Powell, and the grand ole U.S. Senator Wendell Ford of Kentucky. They all spoke eloquently.

As the program continued, I noticed the orchestrator in back of the stage was none other than retired U.S. Congressman Ken Gray. Ken has always been easily recognizable in a crowd with his permed hair, ruddy complexion, bow tie, blue blazer, and white slacks. He glowed almost as much as I did at the Noonday Club. Ken had been out of office for over 30 years, but there he was, still running the show.

When serving in Congress, Ken's nickname was "Prince of Pork." He believed that a congressman's number-one job was to take care of his people back home and bring back facilities and services that they would otherwise not receive. Being from downstate Illinois, he had seen firsthand the poverty and heartache caused by the demise of the coal mines.

So in the late '60s and early '70s, he delivered. Among them were Interstate Highways 57 and 24, and the Rend Lake Conservancy District owned and operated by the U.S. Corps of Engineers, which includes an 18,900-acre lake and 20,000 acres adjoining the lake. The Corp manages water distribution to over sixty southern Illinois communities from the lake. In addition, the State of Illinois has a state park, wildlife areas, land for economic and recreational development, a golf course, motel, marina, and many other amenities around the lake; quite a tribute to Ken.

Ken is a great orator from the old school. He can still talk for hours. On this afternoon, he was the last speaker and gave the best speech of the day, even though there were some really good ones. His ending was the best I've ever heard. I've used it many times since:

"Folks, I've got to leave, and I know you're getting tired of all these speeches. Ole Bill should be here any minute," as he looked at his watch and glanced down the street in the direction the Clinton/Gore motorcade would be approaching. "This kind of reminds me of the time one late Sunday afternoon, when I spoke for a good bit at an old Democratic rally. As the sun was setting, I looked up, and all the people had left except one old man. I looked down at him in his bib-overalls, checkered-flannel, long-sleeved shirt, wide-brimmed hat, high-top boots, and wheat stalk protruding out of the corner of his mouth and asked, 'Old man, what have I said here today that has inspired you to stay until the bitter end?' The old man looked up at me and replied, 'Well, boy, if you'd crawl down off my wagon, I could go home!'"

Epilogue

After reading a preliminary manuscript of this book, a friend responded, "So what?" His response reminded me of the words of one of Peggy Lee's famous songs, "Is That All There Is?" When I inquired of him further he said, "I laughed my butt off." He also said he enjoyed learning more about the Cape Girardeau area and was fascinated by the many characters I wrote about. But he thought the contents spoke to larger issues, and he challenged me to explore them.

Originally, my intent was simply to entertain. As I continued to expand and weave history, local lore, and Midwestern values on the page, what primarily emerged was a portrait of several generations of my family's service to others. It's been said we are a product of our environment. I suppose that's true to a degree. Certainly, our life experiences play major roles in our development. But as individuals, we ultimately have to chart our own courses. We can use our surroundings, family, upbringing, and opportunities as our foundation, success, crutch, excuse, or whatever. In the end, we all have to make choices. Those choices, to a great extent, identify who we are and the values we emulate.

On my father's tombstone are inscribed the words, *His Life Was Public Service*. That's the Ford family mantra: whether aiding the sick and infirmed; inspiring and educating youth; comforting families in their time of need; improving the life of people with disabilities; stepping into the political arena to make our town, county, and state a better place to live; serving in the military; or even something as simple as providing a respite of musical entertainment. Public service is an honorable and noble cause. I'm most proud of my family's legacy of service to others.

So when someone asks, "So what?" My answer is: "In this book, one sees many recipes for respecting one another, helping someone who's less fortunate, and making our world a better place. I challenge others to do the same."

Well, it's time for me "to get down off my wagon" and end this book. Perception is reality too many times in life and politics. Everyone's looking for the quick fix, and often satisfied with sound-bite answers to complex problems. I don't know about you, but I'm tired of the constant yakety-yakety-yak of talk radio and 24-hour TV news broadcasts. I figure there are a lot of you out there, like me, who need a break—a few hours of good chuckles. That's why I related these stories to you. I hope you gained some insight into the days of The Grove. I hope you were entertained. And again, I hope you laughed.

By the way, if you would like to share a story or two, mail them to me:

Jerry Ford
P.O. Box 1088,
Cape Girardeau, MO 63702